RUDE PRAISE

"If preaching feels impossible when grief has no polite language—when rage and protest keep breaking into worship—these sermons are for you. *Rude Praise* refuses to police language, choosing instead to listen, to name sorrow, and to sit in the darkness without rushing to fix it. In these pages, preaching becomes communal—where God's lament meets ours, and no one is left alone."

—Eliana Ah-Rum Ku, Assistant Professor of Homiletics, Graduate School of Practical Theology, South Korea

"Read these sermons if at times you weep for our current world. Read them to be reminded of what great preaching is: filled with rich biblical and contemporary stories, good humor, and smart theological analysis. But most of all, read them because you need good news. Jason Byassee takes psalms of anger and lament and skillfully wrestles from them the joyous gospel of Jesus Christ and what God is doing today."

—Paul Scott Wilson, Professor Emeritus of Homiletics, University of Toronto

"Once upon a time, our greatest theologians—Augustine, Jerome, Luther—preached often on the Psalms. After a hiatus, they're at it again in this elegant volume. Much to ponder and be blessed by here!"

—James C. Howell, Senior Pastor, Myers Park United Methodist Church, Charlotte

"What an extraordinary volume with its invitation into rude praise—as surprising as it is necessary. God invites us to be absolutely honest in our prayers, and this exceptional group of preachers helps us to wrestle with, and then to accept, God's invitation. As they probe some of the harsh and honest words of the Bible, the words of these sermons give us permission to embrace the biblical tradition of rude praise for ourselves and in our time. With endless reasons for lament and anger, for grief and despair swirling around us, this volume offers a pathway forward in prayer that we all need."

—Kristen Deede Johnson, Principal, Wycliffe College, University of Toronto

Rude Praise

Sermons on Poorly Behaved Psalms

Edited by
JASON BYASSEE

CASCADE *Books* • Eugene, Oregon

RUDE PRAISE
Sermons on Poorly Behaved Psalms

Cascade Books
An Imprint of Wipf and Stock Publishers
199 W. 8th Ave., Suite 3
Eugene, OR 97401

www.wipfandstock.com

PAPERBACK ISBN: 979-8-3852-6024-9
HARDCOVER ISBN: 979-8-3852-6025-6
EBOOK ISBN: 979-8-3852-6026-3

Cataloguing-in-Publication data:

Names: Byassee, Jason [editor]. | Andison, Jenny [foreword writer]

Title: Rude praise : sermons on poorly behaved psalms / edited by Jason Byassee.

Description: Eugene, OR: Cascade Books, 2026 | Includes bibliographical references.

Identifiers: ISBN 979-8-3852-6024-9 (paperback) | ISBN 979-8-3852-6025-6 (hardcover) | ISBN 979-8-3852-6026-3 (ebook)

Subjects: LCSH: Bible.—Psalms—Sermons. | Bible.—Psalms—Criticism, interpretation, etc. | Christian ethics. | Bible—Theology.

Classification: BS1430.52 B937 2026 (print) | BS1430.52 (ebook)

For the clergy team at Timothy Eaton Memorial Church:
Dayle, Joanne, and Elaine

Contents

List of Contributors xi

Foreword by Jenny Andison xiii

Acknowledgements xv

Introduction xvii

I. Psalm 2. The God who smashes nations 1
—*Jason Byassee*

II. Psalm 89. The God who hides 9
—*Patrick McManus*

III. Psalm 77. God, did you forget to be merciful? 19
—*Jason Byassee*

IV. Psalm 109. You can't outcurse the Bible 27
—*Jason Byassee*

V. Psalm 149. Boo, other nations! 35
—*Jason Byassee*

VI. Psalm 137. Bashing baby brains 45
—*Jason Byassee*

VII. Psalm 88. The Bible's only tragic ending 55
—*Jason Byassee*

VIII. Psalm 26. Bless me Lord. After all, I deserve it 63
—*Dayle Barrett*

IX. Psalm 58. Hip-hop and rude praise 70
—*Shadrach Kabango*

X. Genesis 18:22–33. Prayer as negotiation: Holy chutzpah! 80
—*Yael Splansky*

XI. Luke 6:27–36. Jesus: Ridiculous and rude 87
—*Jaylynn Byassee*

XII. Psalms 9–10. Good news for the afflicted 96
—*Joseph Mangina*

XIII. Psalm 137. Happy dashers 107
—*Katherine Sonderegger*

XIV. Matthew 25:31–46. Why the end of time matters 112
—*Paul Scott Wilson*

Contributors

Jenny Andison is the rector of St. Paul's Bloor Street and a former area bishop in the Anglican Church of Canada.

Dayle Barrett is an associate pastor at Timothy Eaton Memorial Church in Toronto, ON.

Jason Byassee is the twelfth senior minister of Timothy Eaton Memorial Church.

Jaylynn Byassee is an associate pastor at St. Andrew's Presbyterian Church in Toronto, ON.

Shadrach Kabango, known professionally as Shad K, is a Canadian rapper and broadcaster.

Patrick McManus is the rector of All Saints Kingsway Anglican Church in Toronto.

Joseph Mangina is professor of theology at Wycliffe College at the University of Toronto.

Katherine Sonderegger is professor emeritus of theology at Virginia Theological Seminary in Alexandria.

Paul Scott Wilson is professor emeritus of homiletics at Emmanuel College at the University of Toronto.

Foreword

Jason and I both have big pulpits in Toronto. I mean that in an historic sense—the pulpit at St. Paul's Bloor Street having been donated by a Titanic survivor, and I bet a church named Timothy Eaton Memorial has a pulpit with a story. But just because our pulpits are historic and have hosted notable names over the centuries, doesn't mean we ourselves are effective ministers of the gospel!

So, it was with appropriate personal humility that I approached reading *Rude Praise* recently. Would I be jealous reading my friends winsome and engaging sermons, or would I secretly think "Well, E for effort"? Thankfully the Holy Spirit prevented me from wallowing in either of those sinful thoughts. Instead, I was delighted to feast on sermons that, like the psalms they exegeted and wrestled with, were raw, honest, and sweetly humorous.

Jason has an invitational and sunny (in the sense of shedding great light) way of writing that invites you, the listener, into some wonderful unfolding secret as you immerse yourself in the sermon. Lighthearted anecdotes and whimsical stories from his own life pepper each sermon, but don't let that lull you into a false sense of relaxedness. What I most appreciated about this collection of sermons was how they confronted head on the fact that the Psalms are rarely "nice," many should have "explicit content" warning labels and contain some of the most challenging (repugnant?) passages in the entire Bible. Few of the psalms tackled in this collection would make for good needlepoint or slogans for your mug. In a time when many young adults have walked away from faith because of what they experience as intellectual dishonesty in the church, the frankness of these sermons is bracingly fresh.

Jason is one of the most well-connected people I know, and he uses his easy gift of collegiality to invite some wonderful contributors to this volume. Each in turn wrestle with the "rudeness" of their assigned psalm—honest about the impact of the neglect, or worse, they believe they are experiencing from God. The church has frequently failed to listen carefully to people's real experiences of the ache and confusion of human existence, yet the Psalms do, and this fact shines through the diverse voices in this volume. Read these sermons and be reminded of what people in churches (their friends and co-workers) are actually experiencing. McManus, Barrett, Kabango, Splanksy, Mangina, Sonderegger, and Wilson also allow their own heart of praise, each psalm is a "rude praise" after all, flow out to God, while not neatly tying up each question or outburst of anger in the passages. God is trusted enough in these sermons to be good, if not always clear and obvious.

If you doubt God's existence, these sermons are for you. If it feels like God is hiding God's face from you, read these. If you want help living with some of the most painful parts of the Bible, dip into this volume. If you want to be encouraged by an effective minister of the gospel, Jason Byassee, these sermons will challenge, humor, and then bless you.

"The LORD is my light and my salvation, whom shall I fear?"
Psalm 27:1

Jenny Andison
Rector of St Paul's Bloor Street
and St George's Grange Park, Toronto

Acknowledgements

The obvious people to thank are my fellow preachers whose work fills these pages. Patrick McManus from our sister Anglican church on the westside of Toronto. Dayle Barrett, then a fill-in, now my permanent associate pastor at TEMC. Shadrach Kabango—with all the fancy academic degrees among our authors, none but Shad can claim an Emmy and a Peabody award. Rabbi Yael Splansky, my sister in ministry, from whom I've learned so much. My wife Jaylynn, with whom I am delighted to share all things (but who still won't let me drink after her). Joe Mangina, Toronto's prince of theologians and our erstwhile neighbor. Kate Sonderegger, one of the great systematic theologians living and one of the holiest people I've met. And Paul Scott Wilson, the dean of Canadian preaching, and longtime friend to our congregation. Thank you all for your words and your leadership.

I'm grateful to all those who make preaching at TEMC possible. Blair Smith and Anne Keillor make me and my fellow worship leaders physically audible week by week. Josh del Rosario and Adam Wood make our worship visible via livestream each week. Elaine Choi, John Arndt, and Stephen Boda lead worship. I've heard a stand-up comedian say we preachers do what she never could—we address a gathering that is not at all liquored up. The only way we can do so is that we're worshiped up, with songs as glorious as the ones these friends lead. Our choir leads and volunteers, all those who gather for worship week by week—thank you. I hope you hear yourself reflected in these pages.

I'm grateful too to the folks at Wipf and Stock. I love a publishing house that grows out of a church—the Church of the Servant King, now of blessed memory in Eugene, Oregon. Robin Parry was good enough to ask me what I was up to, I mentioned these sermons, and now here they are. Thank you, friends, not least Charlie Collier for our long, two-decade partnership in the ministry of writing.

Introduction

THESE ARE SOME RUDE sermons you hold in your hands.

Now, of course, these are not really sermons. A sermon is an audible event. It cannot be captured on a page or even in an audio or video recording. These words are, at best, traces of a sermon. God can work through even a trace of the preaching of God's Word, but a sermon properly speaking *takes place* as God's people worship.

In the summer of 2024, we had some rude praise at Timothy Eaton Memorial Church. That is, we tried to learn from the way God's people in scripture speak to God with a kind of outrageous boldness. Rabbi Yael Splansky in these pages calls this scripture's "holy *chutzpah*." A divine daring. The kind that caused Moses to stick his neck out and ask that he be cut off instead of all of Israel (Exod 32:32). The kind that caused Paul to wish he could be cut off for the sake of his people (Rom 9:3). The kind Jesus fleshed in his life and ministry.

Timothy Eaton Church is the sort of downtown old main congregation that once dominated the North American religious landscape. Many such churches have closed, others have dramatically reenvisioned their ministry. TEMC is surprisingly similar in some respects to the ways our forebears worshiped in the early twentieth century. We do choral and organ music. We have a children's choir. We don't hesitate to sing in Latin or to use medieval church music that blesses the Virgin Mary. In other ways we differ—our ushers no longer wear morning coats, our preachers don't always wear robes, and we have a growing contemporary service.

We are a place where a traditional mainline church has a shot at "working."

This is partly surprising because there are some thirteen Christian churches in our neighborhood in Toronto, Ontario, Canada. Thirteen! Forest Hill was once a hot new suburb in Toronto, a hundred odd years ago. Every denomination wanted to claim a plot of land here. Some (here's looking at you, Catholics and Anglicans!) were greedy enough to want two. If we could replant these churches now, we would spread them out liberally around the Greater Toronto Area (GTA, for you novices). But they represent legacies in stone now. They cannot, by definition, simply be uprooted and removed. They are blessedly, stubbornly *here*. We might as well use them for the kingdom's growth, the city's good.

I don't think our Methodist forebears who planted Timothy Eaton could have imagined there would be a day when we'd question the future of the mainline church in North America. They built the behemoth where I serve in 1915 to look like it was built in 1115. If the Vikings invade Toronto, we'll be a fine place to hold out and defend ourselves. Our Gothic style and Ontario stone evoke awe and invite people into relationship with a God beyond our grasp.

We are a congregation of the United Church of Canada, one of those blessed, starry eyed outfits that thought we could undo centuries of Christian division by stitching denominations back together. Similar efforts were made by the Church of South India, the Uniting Church of Australia. Now those are often "lowest common denominator" denominations that believe nothing very distinctive except that when we're in doubt, it's best to tack left. In Canada we were founded in an effort not to compete as colonization moved west—best not to have multiple churches fighting for space in every prairie village, better to work together. We were also founded to compete with Roman Catholics. With newer immigrants from places like Italy and Portugal and Ireland, the fear was that they'd join with English-speaking Canada's old nemesis in Quebec, making a Catholic Canada. It sounds ridiculous now, but history often does.

Now we compete with abject boredom, capitalism, hockey practice, Netflix, and wherever else people are finding their hope these days.

Folks are often surprised at our name. I certainly was, when I first heard it. On reflection, there are churches named for families in various places—Rockefeller Chapel at the University of Chicago, Duke University, Gary Memorial UMC in Wheaton, IL. Eaton's was long known as the department store of choice in Canada. Generations of Canadians went there to shop for their first belt or calculator or dress. It essentially invented the catalogue in Canada. Suddenly families in remote towns deep in the prairies could have access to all the same goods as a shopper in Montreal or Calgary, and the Eaton family made a killing. There are legendary accounts of the Eaton's catalogue providing reading material for folks in outhouses, its crinkled up pages filling in holes against the wind, or filling up hockey players' socks for extra padding. I can assume people of a certain age all shopped at Eaton's, and many worked there. Eaton's closed in the 1990s. A friend joked that I was a real Canadian once I got a job at Eaton's. I joked back: Those are much harder to get now than they once were.

We have done some extraordinary ministry from this spot on St. Clair Avenue. Billy Bishop, Canada's World War I flying ace, was married and buried here. Even some of the family of Eaton's nemesis in the department store business, Simpsons, have worshiped here. Jesus does repair relationships between erstwhile enemies. We host the Churches on the Hill food bank. Legend has it that a neighborhood meeting rose up in opposition to allowing a foodbank in Forest Hill. Who's hungry here? Data showed the need, but that didn't win the room. Retired hockey great Red Kelly did. He stood up and said he liked his neighbors in Forest Hill, but now he was ashamed of every one of them. He'd grown up eating out of foodbanks and soup kitchens. Now that we'd made good enough to live in a fancy neighborhood, how dare we not give of ourselves to help our needier neighbors? The meeting voted unanimously to put the foodbank in. We're one of the busiest in the city now.

I arrived here in 2022 after a longtime and successful pastorate by my predecessor. My charge: to come help TEMC be different. We wanted to be, but we didn't know how. I joke that I'd pastored places with ideas and no money, now I got invited to lead in a place with money and no ideas. It's not entirely true . . . . The pandemic represented a bit of a break between me and my predecessor. And one conviction I got to try out immediately: We need more Old Testament preaching in mainline churches. The lectionary that designates our Bible readings for Sundays has a funneling effect that keeps us preaching from the Synoptic Gospels. These sermons usually go like this: "Jesus is almost as inclusive as we are. Not quite! He still has some racism/sexism/homophobia to overcome. But he's on his way to being as good as we are." And we wonder why folks don't come to our churches.

Since our place has something of a country club reputation (only partially deserved), Old Testament preaching like *Rude Praise* seemed the perfect antidote. I wanted us to learn to pray like the Bible, where some one third of the Psalms are laments—letters to the management—alleging that God is failing at being God. Is there some manager behind the desk here to whom we can make complaint? No? Well, then, we'll complain louder. One could argue that all prayer is rude. It names the gap between the world God wants and the world as it is. And who alone is capable of closing that gap? Precisely the One to whom we raise unanswered prayer.

Since the series happened in the summer, we engaged our traditional practice of inviting outside preachers to leaven the rotation of folks from whom we would hear. So a little more than half the sermons in this book are mine, but the others are by guests. Some of these guests are more in-house—the Rev. Dayle Barrett is now my full-time associate, then he was a fill-in. My wife Jaylynn now pastors at St. Andrew's Presbyterian further downtown. Professor Joe Mangina of Wycliffe College is a colleague at the University of Toronto and turns up for events at TEMC enough to be a near theologian-in-residence. Rabbi Yael Splansky of Holy Blossom Temple has preached and led in our building often—a continuation of our congregations' historic friendship. (Once when

Yael preached here I greeted a female guest who said she was shul shopping, and thought it safer to check Yael out at a church than at her synagogue!) Shadrach Kabango worships with Free Church, a congregation that rents space in TEMC's auditorium and with whom we often partner. Katherine Sonderegger, in addition to being one of the great living theologians, is a friend to our church and to our partner college, Wycliffe. And Paul Scott Wilson, the dean of Canadian preaching, is an annual regular on our docket. No one knows how or why, but he seems to be our annual Labour Day preacher. And Patrick McManus is a recent Wycliffe graduate and outstanding Anglican parish priest in our city. These guests are not strangers—they are more like family. And they one and all leapt at the chance to offer rude praise in our Sunday worship.

Mainline ministers' sermons used to be ubiquitously in print in North America. Newspapers were often founded simply to reprint Sundays' sermons. *Readers Digest* was glad to make them more widely available. Now it is hard to find them. Even Christian publishers and booksellers don't want books of sermons, because people don't buy them. So this book is not just rude; it's a risk. Is there any interest in sermons like these anymore? Our church is still here, after all. We still pursue our mission of influencing all aspects of Canadian culture and society. We still have members of parliament and legislature, titans of industry and judges and lawyers. We also have homeless people and mentally ill people, troubled people and less fortunate people. And some of those . . . are the same people!

They were invited to this bounteous feast of the Word. Now you are too.

CHAPTER I

Psalm 2

The God who smashes nations

Rev. Dr. Jason Byassee

Psalm 2

1 Why do the nations conspire
and the peoples plot in vain?
2 The kings of the earth set themselves,
and the rulers take counsel together
against the LORD and his anointed, saying,
3 "Let us burst their bonds apart
and cast their cords from us."
4 He who sits in the heavens laughs,
the LORD has them in derision.
5 Then he will speak to them in his wrath
and terrify them in his fury, saying,
6 "I have set my king on Zion, my holy hill."
7 I will tell of the decree of the LORD:
He said to me, "You are my son;
today I have begotten you.
8 Ask of me, and I will make the nations your heritage
and the ends of the earth your possession.
9 You shall break them with a rod of iron
and dash them in pieces like a potter's vessel."

[10] Now therefore, O kings, be wise;
be warned, O rulers of the earth.
[11] Serve the Lord with fear;
with trembling kiss his feet,
or he will be angry, and you will perish in the way,
for his wrath is quickly kindled.
Happy are all who take refuge in him.

The Psalms of David are so majestic that they have shaped languages they were not even written in. Their translation into the King James Bible in 1611 still influences not just how you and I talk, but how you and I *think*. My wife Jaylynn had a funeral for a non-churchgoing family once. She asked what scripture they wanted. They said "we want that green pasture stuff." Psalm 23 might be the most famous words in the English language.

But there is another side to the Psalms. For every green pasture and every "from whence cometh my help," there is a psalm full of rancor. For that reason, I want to focus our attention over the following reflections on the often-overlooked "rude praise." When I told our music leadership that I would be preaching the psalms, our director, Dr. Elaine Choi, said "Great, I have loads of music on the psalms." Then I told her which ones. She came back after a search and said, "Uh, sorry, no songs on any of those."

Why focus on these?

So much of our prayer is so polite. "Dear God, if it's not too much trouble, please help us to be even nicer than we already are." These rude psalms pray differently. "God, you are failing at being God. Care to change that, now, please?" As I listen to your lives, I hear so much sorrow. Little polite prayers won't cut it when you face a cross. The answer is these rude psalms. We can pray to God with anger. I didn't grow up in church, but I still think I was somehow taught to be polite when talking to God, like how you're supposed to talk to grandparents. But the Bible is ugly with God. Like how you talk to someone you've lost patience with.

For example, Psalm 2, our psalm for today. This psalm is really important in the history of the church. But I bet you don't know it. God speaks to the nations in wrath, terrifies them with fury, smashes them with a rod of iron, dashes them like a ruined pot. I'm guessing you don't have those verses in needlepoint on a cushion, in crochet your grandma left you.

The Book of Psalms is the longest book in the Bible: 150 poems to God. Some are praise. Some are curses. Some are history. Some lament, tears. They're all there for a reason. They're colors on the palette God wants to paint in our lives. Our organist, Stephen Boda, often dazzles a full house with an organ concert. Our organ has seven thousand pipes, but Stephen says we only use about three-and-a-half thousand normally. These rude praises are the less-used pipes. Those less-used pipes can make a whole symphony of sound.

Psalm 2 has the first word *from God* in the Psalms. What is it? The Lord . . . *laughs*. Isn't that great? The first thing we hear from God in Israel's hymnbook is the sound of laughter. What's the cliché? If you want to make God laugh, tell God your plans. When Sarah our ancestor is told she'll have a baby at age ninety, she does what any sane person that age would do: she laughs. Her baby is called Isaac, which means "he laughs." Laughter, someone wise said, is faith's constant companion. God is the author of humor. Most of Jesus' parables are jokes meant to double us over in laughter, so God can then nudge us into more faithfulness despite ourselves.

This psalm may have started out life for use in the coronation of a new king in Jerusalem.[1] We recently had a coronation in England, so this is familiar. The Kingdom of Judah is at the height of its power. Judah has subjected other nations. Those nations now pay taxes and tribute to Judah's king. And not surprisingly, they resent it. They'd rather *not* pay taxes. They'd rather rebel. And you know, a good time to rebel is when there's a new king. Untested.

Psalm 2 warns them: Don't even think about it. You wouldn't be rebelling against the human king but against the God of Israel who created the worlds. *Those* are the plans God laughs at here.

1. Robert Alter's Psalms translation packs more data about historical critical context into footnotes than whole tomes include in hundreds of pages. See Robert Alter, *The Book of Psalms* (New York: Norton, 2009).

You and I also live in a world where people scheme violence. We see its bitter fruit in Ukraine, Gaza, the USA. Right now, people are planning for evil in ways that will hurt more vulnerable human beings. God has wrath for those who harm the less powerful. I've heard stories in our community of people scammed out of money by those more computer savvy. Scammers prey on loneliness or confusion in new Canadians. Despicable. One of you told me of a woman who married three times, and each time, her husband ended up beating her. God notices, and is furious. We don't usually play on these pipes, use these colors on the palette, but there *is* a place for God's anger. Here's the problem. *We* are not above doing harm ourselves. No one is innocent. So you play with fire when you talk of divine wrath. This psalm plays with fire.

But none of that is why Christians have loved Psalm 2.

Here's why. It speaks of God having a son. *Begetting* that son. An anointed king. Those are really important words in the Christian language. Once we realize Jesus is raised from the dead, and start looking for language to describe who he is, these words take on new meaning. God is also a Son, a begotten one, who is anointed King over the nations.

Now, the words didn't mean all that at first. They referred to Israel's very human king. Those in David's line are sometimes spoken of as God's sons (2 Sam 7:14). The king is really important. But in no way did it mean the king was God. Exodus 4:22 speaks of God's son this way: "*Israel* is my firstborn son." The whole nation, God's child. Sometimes you hear Jesus described as a great moral teacher, but not as God. The great C. S. Lewis said this:

> I am trying here to prevent anyone saying the really foolish thing that people often say about Him: I'm ready to accept Jesus as a great moral teacher, but I don't accept his claim to be God. That is the one thing we must not say. A man who was merely a man and said the sort of things Jesus said would not be a great moral teacher. He would either be a lunatic—on the level with the man who says he is a poached egg—or else he would be the Devil of Hell. You must make your choice. Either this man was, and is, the Son of God, or else a madman or something

> worse. You can shut him up for a fool, you can spit at him and kill him as a demon or you can fall at his feet and call him Lord and God, but let us not come with any patronizing nonsense about his being a great human teacher. He has not left that open to us.[2]

We Christians believe Jesus really is God, so that the word "God" must now be *rethought* to include him. To say that Jesus is God, Lord, anointed, King forever, is not just a religious claim. It is not just true in our hearts or feelings. It is true over the cosmos. Jesus is King over everything that is. You can see it in this psalm:

> 8 Ask of me, and I will make the nations your heritage
> and the ends of the earth your possession.
> be warned, O rulers of the earth. . . .
> 11 Serve the LORD with fear;
> with trembling kiss his feet,
> or he will be angry, and you will perish in the way,
> for his wrath is quickly kindled.

There was a time when Christians looked around Europe and said, "Hmmmm, Psalm 2 is fulfilled. The world is Christian. As far west as Spain or Iceland. As far east as Russia. As far north as Scandinavia. Nothing but rulers submitted to Christ, ruling under the sign of the cross." Now we knew vaguely there were Muslims beyond Christian Europe. And we knew there were Jews in some places ruled by Christians. So some Christian rulers tried to change that. *Demand* the Jews convert. March off to Jerusalem and retake it. Make the world Christian by force. You know about Columbus sailing the ocean blue in 1492. You know what else happened that year in Spain? Christians reconquered the Iberian Peninsula from Muslims and kicked out all Jews. Ferdinand and Isabela are still called Los Reyes Católicos in Spain, the Catholic monarchs. They *made* Spain uniformly Christian in 1492.

We Protestants used to say, yeah that's just Catholics misbehaving. But all Christians have all been guilty of using violence to make the world right. And not just Christians—our wars today are

2. C. S. Lewis, *Mere Christianity* (San Francisco: Harper, 2023), 40–41.

fought for democracy, capitalism, human rights. We still have crusades; we just call them sanitized words. In World War I, Europe was still Christian enough that both sides, Allied and Central powers, saw the war as a crusade—against other Christians,[3] trying to make the world the one Psalm 2 imagines by using violence.

We have done great damage trying to live out this scripture with its political imagination of conformity.

What do we do instead?

Point out ways, places, where Christ rules without violence and where you can even see it.

In 1988 the world was divided between ruling powers: East and West. Both armed to the teeth with nuclear weapons. Most of us in here grew up with drills in schools in case of nuclear war: get under desks, cover our heads. Then in 1989 something else happened. The Berlin Wall fell without any violence at all. East and West Germany later merged back into one. Countries abandoned the Soviet Union, and it *dissolved*. From the end of World War II in 1945 until 1989, we had all *planned* for war. And instead, we got a non-violent revolution. In Czechoslovakia they called it the *Velvet* Revolution because it was so smooth. And in East Germany, it was prayer meetings that led the way. Protestors gathered at St. Nicholas Church in Leipzig with candles. First a few dozen. Then a few hundred. Then a few thousand. Then a few hundred thousand. The East German Stasi secret police didn't know what to do. They were ready for tanks, not for candles. And the world was changed. No one saw it coming. No one would have believed it if you told them it was coming. Until it did.[4]

For more than a thousand years, we Christians assumed Christ would rule through violence. But maybe Christ rules without weapons? And sometimes you can even see it?

Our Christian forebears were not wrong to think that the church is political. Anytime you speak of power, rule, authority, you're talking politics, as this psalm does. But we were wrong to

3. Philip Jenkins, *The Great and Holy War* (San Francisco: Harper, 2014).

4. *The Prayers for Peace at St. Nicholas Church in Leipzig* (Leipzig: Evangelisch-Lutherische Kirchgemeinde, 2020).

think that politics has to be violent. That God wants us to *inflict* the kingdom on others at the point of a sword. Jesus commands us to love enemies. That means learning from and respecting them. He's bringing his kingdom *that* way. By cross and resurrection, not by gun or nuke.

The psalm ends this way: God's "wrath is quickly kindled." Can you think of a verse that sounds different? A verse that has been called the John 3:16 of the Old Testament? It's Exodus 34:6

> The LORD, the LORD,
> a God merciful and gracious,
> slow to anger,
> and abounding in steadfast love.

But which is it? Is God's wrath "quickly kindled?" Or is the Lord "slow to anger?" You know where I'm going with this don't you? Both. They're both pipes in the organ; colors on the palette. Sometimes we need to say God's wrath is quickly kindled: for those in bondage; for the six million lost in the holocaust; for the children of Gaza now; for the millions of Africans stolen and lost in the middle passage. God remembers, and acts, and will make things right with justice. *And* God is slow to anger, abounding in steadfast love. Because without that, there is no hope for any of us. We all oppress, do harm, fall short. And God's patience with us is a cross. Arms out in embrace, absorbing our violence, giving us back peace, even before we ask.

At our best, we Christians have always known that God rules through *martyrdom*. The *way* God conquers the nations is through us laying down our own lives. Not taking others' lives. I know that's paradoxical, and I can't explain it to you fully. But here's a story. The early church celebrated the story of the forty martyrs of Sebaste. It's a little legendary. Under persecution by a Roman emperor, forty Christian soldiers were set out on a frozen lake to freeze to death. The pagan soldiers on shore lit up a fire and said you can come and live if you just renounce Christ. One did, to save his skin. But then a soldier guarding them saw their faith, threw off his clothes too, and joined them on the lake to die. That pitiful freezing army of martyrs is more powerful naked than when they wore armor, or dealt out death.

In this series on rude praise, we learn to pray like the psalmist: God laughs at human schemes for power. Because God *is* all the power there is. And God's power spends itself in love. Only and always in love. Amen.

CHAPTER II

Psalm 89

The God who hides

Rev. Dr. Patrick McManus

Psalm 89

A Maskil of Ethan the Ezrahite.
1 I will sing of your steadfast love, O LORD, forever;
with my mouth I will proclaim your faithfulness to all generations.
2 I declare that your steadfast love is established forever;
your faithfulness is as firm as the heavens.

3 You said, "I have made a covenant with my chosen one;
I have sworn to my servant David:
4 'I will establish your descendants forever
and build your throne for all generations.'" *Selah*

5 Let the heavens praise your wonders, O LORD,
your faithfulness in the assembly of the holy ones.
6 For who in the skies can be compared to the LORD?
Who among the heavenly beings is like the LORD,
7 a God feared in the council of the holy ones,
great and awesome above all who are around him?
8 O LORD God of hosts,
who is as mighty as you, O LORD?

Your faithfulness surrounds you.
9 You rule the raging of the sea;
when its waves rise, you still them.
10 You crushed Rahab like a carcass;
you scattered your enemies with your mighty arm.
11 The heavens are yours; the earth also is yours;
the world and all that is in it—you founded them.
12 The north and the south—you created them;
Tabor and Hermon joyously praise your name.
13 You have a mighty arm;
strong is your hand, high your right hand.
14 Righteousness and justice are the foundation of your throne;
steadfast love and faithfulness go before you.
15 Happy are the people who know the festal shout,
who walk, O LORD, in the light of your countenance;
16 they exult in your name all day long
and extol your righteousness.
17 For you are the glory of their strength;
by your favor our horn is exalted.
18 For our shield belongs to the LORD,
our king to the Holy One of Israel.

19 Then you spoke in a vision to your faithful one and said,
"I have set the crown on one who is mighty;
I have exalted one chosen from the people.
20 I have found my servant David;
with my holy oil I have anointed him;
21 my hand shall always remain with him;
my arm also shall strengthen him.
22 The enemy shall not outwit him;
the wicked shall not humble him.
23 I will crush his foes before him
and strike down those who hate him.
24 My faithfulness and steadfast love shall be with him,
and in my name his horn shall be exalted.
25 I will set his hand on the sea
and his right hand on the rivers.
26 He shall cry to me, 'You are my Father,
my God, and the Rock of my salvation!'
27 I will make him the firstborn,
the highest of the kings of the earth.

28 Forever I will keep my steadfast love for him,
and my covenant with him will stand firm.
29 I will establish his line forever
and his throne as long as the heavens endure.
30 If his children forsake my law
and do not walk according to my ordinances,
31 if they violate my statutes
and do not keep my commandments,
32 then I will punish their transgression with the rod
and their iniquity with scourges,
33 but I will not remove from him my steadfast love
or be false to my faithfulness.
34 I will not violate my covenant
or alter the word that went forth from my lips.
35 Once and for all I have sworn by my holiness;
I will not lie to David.
36 His line shall continue forever,
and his throne endure before me like the sun.
37 It shall be established forever like the moon,
an enduring witness in the skies." *Selah*

38 But now you have spurned and rejected him;
you are full of wrath against your anointed.
39 You have renounced the covenant with your servant;
you have defiled his crown in the dust.
40 You have broken through all his walls;
you have laid his strongholds in ruins.
41 All who pass by plunder him;
he has become the scorn of his neighbors.
42 You have exalted the right hand of his foes;
you have made all his enemies rejoice.
43 Moreover, you have turned back the edge of his sword,
and you have not supported him in battle.
44 You have removed the scepter from his hand
and hurled his throne to the ground.
45 You have cut short the days of his youth;
you have covered him with shame. *Selah*

46 How long, O LORD? Will you hide yourself forever?
How long will your wrath burn like fire?
47 Remember how short my time is—

for what vanity you have created all mortals!
48 Who can live and never see death?
Who can escape the power of Sheol? *Selah*

49 Lord, where is your steadfast love of old,
which by your faithfulness you swore to David?
50 Remember, O Lord, how your servant is taunted,
how I bear in my bosom the insults of the peoples,
51 with which your enemies taunt, O Lord,
with which they taunted the footsteps of your anointed.

52 Blessed be the Lord forever.
Amen and Amen.

You are a wild God. When we think we've got you boxed in, you break out of our small idolatries, you expand our imaginations and alight them with your grace. Burn us with your presence, speak to us in your Word and transform us for the sake of him who endured abandonment, your Son, Jesus Christ. Amen.

These psalms, if we let them, bare their teeth and show themselves to be something other than the sentimentalized thing they have become in many a mainline tradition. They are not nice prayers. If we attend to them with some intention, we can hear them again as these intimate, hard, guttural, raw, and deeply faithful prayers that can sound rather blasphemous to our modern ears. They are psalms that aren't afraid to roll up their sleeves and contend with God to wrestle a blessing out of him.

Now, I'm an Anglican preacher, which means I'm a lectionary preacher. I didn't grow up with the lectionary, so I came to it later in life. I've been a lectionary preacher now for the past seventeen years and rarely have I strayed from it. The lectionary, shared by churches around the world, is a three-year cycle of selected readings that are assigned for given Sundays throughout the liturgical year. It is a marvel and I think a gift to the church, but lots of Scripture gets ignored. Don't get me wrong, I appreciate the rhythm of readings and the care that has gone into producing the selection of readings through the years. And yet, we're human, and there are scriptures we just don't like or portions of Scripture we'd rather avoid. There's language and images and stories that make us feel uncomfortable, that offend our rather sensitive souls.

So, believe me when I tell you that it is a joy and an adventure to preach off lectionary when I get the chance, and particularly exciting for me to dig into this rude psalm where this faithful songwriter speaks to God with a tenacity and doggedness that can come across as an offensive prayer.

In our last chapter, you all met the God who smashes nations, who in the Son's cross bears forth the only power that matters, the power of God that spends itself entirely and fully in love. Well, in Psalm 89, we meet the God who disappears, the God who hides, the God who is MIA, and we meet this psalmist who calls him out on it in prayer.

I had a lovely professor of theology, David Demson, who studied with the great Swiss theologian Karl Barth.[1] One day we were dealing with a particularly nasty part of the book of Jeremiah where it spoke of God's wrath coming upon God's people and one well-intentioned student piped up and said, "Dr. Demson, Jeremiah just doesn't speak to me," to which he responded without missing a beat, "Frankly, I don't blame him." We tend to approach the Scriptures in the same way: We like what we like, and we don't what we don't. And what we don't like, we don't have the foggiest idea of what to do with, so we tend to ignore and focus on the bits we do like.

Thomas Jefferson, the third president of the United States, had a habit of playing at Christianity. He used to sit at his desk with the Scriptures in front of him and he would take a sharp knife and basically cut out bits of text on the page. The parts he liked, he would paste back together, and the rest he left on the cutting room floor, chaff excised for the kernel of what he thought the good stuff. While not many of us sit and try to write our own Bibles, we do

1. Note from Jason: What the preacher, Father Patrick, did not know was that Professor Demson, now of blessed memory, had been attending our church for some time and was there that morning.

tend to ignore, or at least flout, the parts we don't like to hear or don't know what to do with.

Psalm 89—a psalm I'm guessing you're not too familiar with—only appears in the lectionary twice. Once in Advent and once in Ordinary time. On both occasions, the lectionary is very selective as to what it cuts and pastes and what it leaves out. In the lectionary readings of it we never get verses 38 to the end of the psalm, so it comes off as a psalm of wonderful delight in and praise of God and God's faithfulness. Without the end, the psalm seems pretty rosy, but as we heard this morning, that's not the whole psalm, that's not the whole story, that's not how the psalm ends.

It is a longer psalm that spends two-thirds of its length extolling and praising God for his goodness, faithfulness, and trustworthiness. Frankly, it sounds just awesome: "I will sing of your steadfast love, O Lord, forever; with my mouth I will proclaim your faithfulness to all generations. I declare that your steadfast love is established forever; your faithfulness is as firm as the heavens."

That's what we do in our church's worship, and it's something some churches do very well: sing of God's steadfast love. Fitting for us that this psalm is credited to a music leader in the court, to a fellow named Ethan the Ezrahite who was tasked with leading the congregation in song. This is his psalm, his song, his prayer about David and praising God for all the goodness he's shown in the life of King David. He spends most of the psalm extolling God for God's promises to uphold and defend David's rule and his kingdom. He praises God for prospering David and his line: "I have found my servant David; with my holy oil I have anointed him; my hand shall always remain with him; my arm also shall strengthen him. The enemy shall not outwit him; the wicked shall not humble him. . . . I will establish his line forever and his throne as long as the heavens endure." Sounds like a God kind of thing to say, right? The Scriptures are full of these promises.

But. But there's a but in verse 38, and it's a pretty big but. Take a look at it. "But" you have abandoned him; "but" you have spurned your anointed; "but" you have rejected your covenant with him and left him alone; "but" you have left his crown in the dust, the crown that you put on his head, and now he is taunted, scorned by those who pass him by. It's a pretty big but, and the whole psalm turns on it.

Life turns on these big buts doesn't it? "But" you lost your job; "but" you have cancer; "but" your marriage is in trouble; but, but, but. Buts have amazing power over us; they can devastate us, and they can crush us, making us to feel abandoned by God, and they can leave us nowhere else to turn save to these hard prayers to a hidden God, prayers from a deep place, wondering if we should even give them voice, wondering if God is around to even hear them.

Historically, the best we can tell is that this "but" has to do with some significant, devastating historical occurrence that upended the Davidic line. It could have been the original division of the kingdom and its twelve tribes into two kingdoms between the north and the south, between Israel and Judah, or maybe it was the death of Josiah and the apparent end of the line of David. Whatever it was, for this songwriter, it was devastating, world-altering stuff that hit him and the people of God in the gut. All that David had worked for seemed to be thrown into the waste bin of history. King David, amazing man of God, "but" his line is threatened, and he is scorned and spurned.

This is a psalm that the Old Testament scholar Walter Brueggemann calls "a psalm of disorientation."[2] It is a psalm that gives voice to that feeling of your world being flipped upside-down, and not in a good way. It's the dissonance and disorientation you feel when the floor falls out from underneath you.

Yet, instead of turning his attention to the situation and focusing on the "what ifs" and "what if nots," this psalmist directs his anger and his disorientation directly to God. This is strong language! The psalmist accuses God of disappearing, of exiting stage left of the great narrative of salvation and abandoning them. It's a scene that rivals Beckett's *Waiting for Godot*; here's the psalmist

2. Walter Brueggemann, *The Message of the Psalms: A Theological Commentary* (Minneapolis: Fortress, 1985).

sitting in the midst of the scourges of his life and he whistles into the dark, dizzying emptiness and cries out to this God who hides, "How long, O Lord? Will you hide yourself forever?"

It is, biblically, a question for those who wrestle with God and who wonder if the Lord is with them, because everything around them looks to be evidence that the Lord is not. But it's never a complaint into the ether. It's a complaint directed to God in prayer, and there's a huge difference.

Think about Job, who exclaims:

> If I go forward, he is not there;
> or backward, I cannot perceive him;
> on the left he hides, and I cannot behold him;
> I turn to the right, but I cannot see him. (23:8–9)

Or think about Isaiah who says at one point: "You are a God who hides himself" (Isa 45:15). And unless you think this is simply about our feelings or psychological projections, remember in Isaiah where God tells his people: "For a while I have abandoned you, but with great compassion, I will gather you" (Isa 54:7). God hides.

To pray to a God like this—one who hides and leaves the picture; something we particularly feel during dark times of struggle or in the midst of suffering—takes patience, it takes determination, it takes resilience; it takes faith! To pray to God and ask in anger if he's ever going to show up for you again is not a prayer for the faint of heart, *but it is a prayer*, prayed by the faithful constantly and consistently. If you haven't been there in your life needing a prayer like this one, you will be, and I pray that this prayer will be on your lips and in your heart.

To ask the question with this psalmist, "how long O Lord, will you hide yourself forever?" is hard. It's a difficult question to ask, but it is asked by those who genuinely wrestle with God. Just as only a lover can know what it means to be abandoned by their beloved, only a God-obsessed people can know what it means to be abandoned by God.

The apathetic among us may never come to ask such a question, but when the chips are down and everywhere you look seems to be more evidence of the absence of God, this will become for you a holy question, a question you will ask with those who have gone before you, like Job, like Isaiah, like this Ethan the Ezrahite. Praise the Lord—yes, I know I'm supposed to do that, but where is he? I can't find him, this wily, hidden God. Our sufferings or the commonplace tragedies of our mundane lives seem at times to be the only thing we see, abandoned to the crush of circumstance, with God nowhere in sight.

Shortly after Mother Theresa died, her journals were published.[3] People were shocked by the depth of despair she expressed in them. She experienced years and years of feeling abandoned by God, asking the question constantly, where are you God? And she got nothing in reply. I think folks were shocked because we tend to falsely associate holiness with certitude. But she kept loving and caring between the answers, learning to wrestle with this question, and loving throughout the silences of her life.

I think that's what the Christian life is. A wrestling with God. A holy contention. A loving in between the silences. That's how these psalms teach us to pray: not with the niceties and conventions of our pleasant social interactions but with the passion and grit that it takes to contend with God. Remember that this is where Israel gets his name, as Jacob wrestled with God. The whole identity of God's people is as a people who wrestle, who contend, who struggle with God (Gen 32:22–32). And yes, God acts, and yes, God saves, but not by erasing the conflict, not by taking them out of it, but by wandering in it with them, by meeting them in the middle of it.

This is a God who will hide under the shadow of the cross, for the foolish and weak to find him there, for the threadbare to be clothed there with the splendid mysteries of God's grace. "My God, My God, Why have you forsaken me?" "My God, where are you?" Jesus presents this psalm all over again in his life, death, and new life. He is the one in whom these rude psalms and prayers find

3. Mother Teresa, *Come Be My Light: The Private Writings of the Saint of Calcutta* (New York: Image, 2009).

their end and their beginning. Because they are on his lips, they ought to be on ours.

To find him in this weakness and discover that it's God's strength, to find him in the foolishness of this cross and discover that it is God's wisdom, that is the delight of the Christian life; it is the revelation of the grain of the universe! To find out that this God-forsaken place, and this God-forsaken crucified one, is actually the fullness of God's presence is the power of the gospel for the salvation of this world. This is the hidden God found ruling from a cross; this is the goodness of the good news of the gospel; the Son of God goes the way of this abandonment for us finally, and fully, and faithfully, so that we can go to the God-forsaken people and places of this world and the God-forsaken corners of our lives with the glory of his presence.

So, pray this psalm when God hides from you. You don't pray it alone. You cannot pray it alone. It is the psalmist's prayer; it is the prayer of our Lord from the cross; it is Israel's prayer; it is the church's prayer. So pray when you feel abandoned to circumstance. Pray this psalm in the midst of whatever crushes you. Friends, struggle with this God and wrestle a blessing from him.

Amen.

CHAPTER III

Psalm 77

God, did you forget to be merciful?

Jason Byassee

Psalm 77

1 I cry aloud to God,
aloud to God, that he may hear me.
2 In the day of my trouble I seek the Lord;
in the night my hand is stretched out without wearying;
my soul refuses to be comforted.
3 I think of God, and I moan;
I meditate, and my spirit faints. *Selah*
4 You keep my eyelids from closing;
I am so troubled that I cannot speak.
5 I consider the days of old
and remember the years of long ago.
6 I commune with my heart in the night;
I meditate and search my spirit;
7 "Will the Lord spurn forever
and never again be favorable?
8 Has his steadfast love ceased forever?
Are his promises at an end for all time?
9 Has God forgotten to be gracious?
Has he in his anger shut up his compassion?" *Selah*

10 And I say "It is my grief
that the right hand of the Most High has changed."
11 I will call to mind the deeds of the Lord;
I will remember your wonders of old.
12 I will meditate on all your work
and muse on your mighty deeds.
13 Your way, O God, is holy
What god is so great as our God?
14 You are the God who works wonders;
you have displayed your might among the peoples.
15 With your strong arm you redeemed your people,
the descendants of Jacob and Joseph. *Selah*
16 When the waters saw you, O God,
when the waters saw you, they were afraid;
the very deep trembled.
17 The clouds poured out water;
the skies thundered;
your arrows flashed on every side.
18 The crash of your thunder was in the whirlwind;
your lightnings lit up the world;
the earth trembled and shook.
19 Your way was through the sea,
your path through the mighty waters,
yet your footprints were unseen.
20 You led your people like a flock
by the hand of Moses and Aaron.

Somewhere along the way you can get the impression that if we are going to talk to God, we had better be polite. Say please and thank you. Don't raise your voice. Be pleasant. Sit up straight. Use proper grammar. Be good girls and boys, or God won't answer. In other words, treat God like Santa Claus.

I don't know where we get this impression. But I do know one place it does not come from. It does not come from the Bible.

The Psalms are Israel's hymnal. They are 150 poems that do many things. They celebrate. They complain. They bless. They also curse. One thing they never are is nice. If the Psalms wrote out a Christmas list they'd get back a lump of coal. If we're going to speak to God the way the Psalms do, we could be a little rude. Or a lot.

In this series of reflections on rude praise, we're paying attention to those psalms that misbehave. Something like a third of the Psalms are laments. If we pray to God the way the Bible prays to God then one third of our prayers will also be complaints. "Hey, God, you're doing a bad job of being God. Do better!" St. Teresa of Avila in sixteenth-century Spain was thrown from her carriage one time, and landed in a ditch in the mud. She'd been praying when it happened. She shouted "God if this is how you treat your friends, it's no wonder you have so few!" That's the prayer of someone reading the Bible well.

Take for example Psalm 77. Look at some of the verbs used to describe prayer: I cry aloud. I moan. My spirit faints. I am so troubled. I cannot speak. God used to be good, but no more. This is not polite language. This is more like the language of an athlete spleening to the referee. "Are you blind!? Are you serious!?" But the psalmist is just getting warmed up.

> 7 Will the Lord spurn forever
> and never again be favorable?
> 8 Has his steadfast love ceased forever?
> Are his promises at an end for all time?
> 9 Has God forgotten to be gracious?

This is the prayer of someone betrayed. She takes some of the most cherished descriptions of God—that God is good, that God loves, that God keeps promises, that God is gracious—and puts them all in the interrogative mood. "Really? You sure? I mean, you payin' attention?" Talk this way to your spouse, and you'll find yourself single. Try talking this way to your father and find somewhere else to go for Christmas. Happy father's day, by the way.[1]

What's going on here? And how can we learn from it?

We sometimes call them the Psalms of David, but most of them are much later than the time of King David himself. Even the ones that say David wrote them were likely only written down centuries later. David's was a time of grandeur for Israel: defeating enemies, prosperity, a high tide of national pride. But by the

1. I'll let you guess what day this was preached on.

time many of the psalms were written down, those times were long gone. In fact, there was no king in Israel anymore. There was no Israel anymore—its northern kingdom had been destroyed by the Assyrians in 722 BC and Judah, the two southern tribes around Jerusalem, had been conquered in 586 BC by the Babylonians. God's people were down to a rump of their old selves, just two tribes of the original twelve, and even those were carted off to miserable exile far from home: no temple, no promised land, no king, no, no, no. So the psalmist demands an explanation. "So . . . you promised a king forever. A promised land forever. Freedom from slavery forever. To be our God forever. But here we are, no king, no land, no freedom—does that mean no God?"

Can you see why the psalmist is being impolite?

In the great musical *Fiddler on the Roof*, the main character Tevye complains about how God's chosen people are always mistreated. "God, if this is how you treat your chosen, couldn't you choose someone else? We've had enough." More seriously now, think of how our Jewish elder siblings must have prayed in the Holocaust: "You call us your child, your bride, yet our enemies burn us down to the nub." David Weiss Halivni was a rabbi who survived the holocaust. He opens his memoir *The Book and the Sword* with this story.

> When the sound of the closing of the door, after the first child was shoved into the crematorium, reached heaven, Michael, the most beneficent of angels, could not contain himself and angrily approached God. Michael asked, "Do You now pour out Your wrath upon children?" . . . God, piqued by Michael's insolence, shouted back at him, "I am the Lord of the Universe. If you are displeased with the way I conduct the world, I will return it to void and null." . . . Michael went back to his place, ashen and dejected, but could not resist looking back sheepishly at God and saw a huge tear rolling down His face, destined for the legendary cup which collects tears, and which, when full, will bring the redemption of the world.[2]

2. David Weiss Halivni, *The Book and the Sword: A Life of Learning in the Shadow of Destruction* (New York: Farrar: 1996), 3.

That's a searing prayer. Way past impolite into another realm altogether.

Halfway through the psalm, there is a pivot. Like the psalmist has made a decision and is going to go another way.

> 11 I will call to mind the deeds of the LORD;
> I will remember your wonders of old.
> 12 I will meditate on all your work
> and muse on your mighty deeds.

"Ok, God, you're not keeping up your end of the bargain. You're failing at being God. But I'm not going to fail as a disciple. In fact, I'm going to call to mind your deeds. Remember your wonders of old. Meditate on your work. I'm going to do my part, God. Maybe then you'll remember to do yours."[3] The psalmist is like the spouse who determines to stick in there with the marriage even when the partner doesn't deserve it. I used to tell this story to my preaching students in Vancouver: It's of a sermon in a Black church. Not a very good sermon. The preacher hadn't taken the time to prepare and knew the sermon was terrible. But one older member wasn't having it. "Amen!" She shouted. "Preach! Praise the Lord!" He finally limped to a merciful conclusion and asked this sister on her way out, "Why were you carrying on like that? You and I both know that wasn't a very good sermon." "Oh honey," she said. "Just because you weren't doing your job doesn't mean I'm not going to do mine." That's the psalmist's word to God: "Oh God, just because you're not doing your job doesn't mean I'm not going to do mine."

It's as though the psalmist is going to remind God how to be God. "Maybe there's some muscle memory in there for you God. Maybe if I start the song, your Alzheimer's-addled brain will join in. Maybe if I start to lead the dance, your feet will remember the steps and you'll waltz along with me."

> 14 You are the God who works wonders;
> you have displayed your might among the peoples.
> 15 With your strong arm you redeemed your people,

3. Despite the quote marks, I don't usually speak this way to God. But to listen to these Psalms, why shouldn't I!?

the descendants of Jacob and Joseph.

"Remember that God? Yeah that was cool. But you don't do that sort of thing anymore now, do you? Couldn't you again? I mean, if I praise you enough, maybe you'll remember to be faithful? Just one more time, for old time's sake?"

This is the perfect word for you if you're not sure where God is in your life. If you're stuck, like Israel of old, between an attacking army of Egyptians in one direction and a sea of death in the other. If there's no way out. Death that way . . . and death that way. Or more mundanely, if God's not answering your prayers. Remember God's merciful deeds of old. Recount God's works in the past. "Hey, remember, God? You used to help me out in times like this. Could you do that again, God? Come on, put your hand here, your other hand here, now let's move to the music shall we? You'll remember, won't you, God?"

Sigmund Freud said the most important day in a man's life is the day his father dies. I don't know what Freud meant by it. I assume he meant something I wouldn't approve of. But I know when people lose their fathers and I quote that to them, they nod with recognition. Yes, this is an important day. Whether theirs were good fathers or not, loving fathers or not, they were at least alive—there. It was possible to appeal to them for help. But with no father, it's like we're orphaned, however old we are. All the responsibility falls on us. There's no one else around to be the grown-up. My dad is still living, but I still think of things he did long ago. He taught me basketball; whatever sense of humor I have; how to triage a crisis. But fatherhood is more than biology. I think of the handful of mentors I've had. This one taught me how to listen. The other how to say I'm sorry. If your fathers or mentors are still living, call them up today and say thanks. And if not, if they live in God's presence and not in ours, give God thanks for them. And if you lament not having that, if there's a hole in your life where a good dad should have been, I'm so sorry. Ask God to be that Father for you, that Mother for you. And maybe even dare to ask God, "Hey, why didn't you give me that? Would've been nice."

The psalmist continues:

[16] When the waters saw you, O God,
when the waters saw you, they were afraid;
the very deep trembled.
[17] The clouds poured out water;
the skies thundered;
your arrows flashed on every side.
[18] The crash of your thunder was in the whirlwind;
your lightnings lit up the world;
the earth trembled and shook.
[19] Your way was through the sea,
your path through the mighty waters.

She's remembering the exodus. "God, you used to make the weather fight against the Egyptians. Thunder and lightning and earthquake and ocean. When we had no army, God, you were our army. Pharaoh and his slavers had no chance. Creation belongs to you, God, and you fought against Egypt."

At Passover Seders, where Jews recount the exodus, they enter the story. At a friend's table, they go around and say when they've experienced Egypt that year. The word "Egypt" in Jewish vocabulary is synonymous with trouble, distress, anxiety. *Mitzrayim* is how you say it in Hebrew. Say that with me: *Mitzrayim*. Good, you're speaking God's language. What's been your *Mitzrayim* this year? At the table, one nephew said he'd gotten divorced that year—a family cut in half. *Mitrayim*. A granddaughter stood up and said she'd gone through puberty that year. Yep, that's in no way easy. *Mitzrayim*. Do you see what they're doing? They're remembering that God has led people out of Egypt before. And God will do it again. "We've been in trouble before, and God, you delivered. You know what to do with *Mitzrayim*, don't you, God?"

I was in the Netherlands for a conference on preaching. I noticed the city flag in Amsterdam. It looks like some sort of graphic on a game show when the player fails. The three X's are actually for three disasters: one for the plague in the Middle Ages; two for a great fire that burned Amsterdam; and three for the invasion of Napoleon. Now that's a proper city symbol. We been burnt before. Conquered before. But we're still here. If you ask someone about their tattoos, they're often reminders of some tragedy in their lives.

This is for someone I lost. Some disaster I overcame. Like X's on the flag. I've found the worst moments in my life are also the seedbeds for the best. When I was fifteen years old, I was cut from my school's basketball team. Basketball was my whole identity. I cried for days. But the first Christian group I ever led met at the same time as basketball practice. I could never have attended if I were playing. The thing that I thought ended my life had sort of begun it.

When Mt. St. Helen's erupted in Oregon an entire region was changed. Scientists said it would be half a century before anything would grow there again. As it turned out, they were wrong. That ecological landscape is perfect for preserving seeds. And some of those seeds only bloom after fire. So when it burned, those seeds were released and bloomed.[4] As a preacher friend of mine in Holland pointed out, that'll preach. The cross is bad. But there is no resurrection without it.

Now don't let God off the hook for this. Here's what I'm not saying. Friedrich Nietzsche famously said, "Whatever doesn't kill you makes you stronger." Uh, no. This is not "grit your teeth, tough it out, and come out better for it." That's not what the Bible is saying at all. Here's what the Bible is saying: "God, are you listening? Because if you are, you're doing a bad job at being God. Here, let me remind you. This is how it works. I praise you for your deeds of old. And you do a new thing now. Like those old deeds, remember? Like exodus. Like resurrection. And do it, like, now, OK? We're waiting, God. It's time for you to act." Amen.

4. I owe this move to Dan Matheson, late of Tenth Church in Vancouver, BC.

CHAPTER IV

Psalm 109

You can't out-curse the Bible

Jason Byassee

Psalm 109:6–19, 26–31

6 They say, "Appoint a wicked man against him;
let an accuser stand on his right.
7 When he is tried, let him be found guilty;
let his prayer be counted as sin.
8 May his days be few;
may another seize his position.
9 May his children be orphans
and his wife a widow.
10 May his children wander about and beg;
may they be driven out of the ruins they inhabit.
11 May the creditor seize all that he has;
may strangers plunder the fruits of his toil.
12 May there be no one to do him a kindness
nor anyone to pity his orphaned children.
13 May his posterity be cut off;
may his name be blotted out in the second generation.
14 May the iniquity of his father be remembered before the LORD,
and do not let the sin of his mother be blotted out.

[15] Let them be before the Lord continually,
and may his memory be cut off from the earth.
[16] For he did not remember to show kindness
but pursued the poor and needy
and the brokenhearted to their death.
[17] He loved to curse; let curses come on him.
he did not like blessing; may it be far from him.
[18] He clothed himself with cursing as his coat;
may it soak into his body like water,
like oil into his bones.
[19] May it be like a garment that he wraps around himself,
like a belt that he wears every day." . . .

[26] Help me, O Lord my God!
Save me according to your steadfast love.
[27] Let them know that this is your hand;
you, O Lord, have done it.
[28] Let them curse, but you will bless.
Let my assailants be put to shame, may your servant be glad.
[29] May my accusers be clothed with dishonor;
may they be wrapped in their own shame as in a mantle.
[30] With my mouth I will give great thanks to the Lord;
I will praise him in the midst of the throng.
[31] For he stands at the right hand of the needy,
to save them from those who would condemn them to death.

When I pastored in North Carolina, I had a lot of former Baptists. The South is where there are more Baptists than people, so if someone new joined us they likely had been Baptists at some point. I never liked taking members from some other church, just moving sheep around. It's one reason I moved to Canada: There are no Baptists left to steal here. Anyway, they brought a phrase with them from Baptist-land. They would say, "You can't out-give God." However much money you give to the church, God will give you more back. In one way I agree: Generosity begets generosity. I ran the phrase by a financial planner, and he said they're probably right. If you give more to the church, you'll have to take better care of the rest, and you'll grow it. In another way I'd disagree. To say "You can't out-give God" sounds like *however* much you give, God will give you more back. That's no sacrifice. It's an investment strategy. So I'm still wrestling with this phrase, but I think there's insight here: You can't out-give God.

This reflection is called "You can't out-curse the Bible"; we might as well call it "You can't out-curse God." When most people think of cursing and the church, they think we're against it. Naughty words from the bathroom or the bedroom. Who cares? That's not the sort of curse we're talking about. Here's the sort of curse we're against: I was skiing in BC, and there was a skier even less adept than me, new to the sport, who looked Asian. She got in someone's way, and the someone, assuming the Asian woman didn't speak English, shouted: "I hope you fall down, hit your head, and die." *That's* a curse. Some cultures know better than to say such things out loud. Words have power. They can *effect* what they say. And not necessarily for their intended target—they can boomerang back around and land on the curser. Jesus commands us not to speak hateful things or even to hate another person at all. Good luck with that. Even when someone curses, Jesus commands, you should bless them in return.

Well, Psalm 109 is a curse to end all curses. It would make a sailor blush, a stand-up comedian cover their ears. Marilyn Manson, who is a sort of shock artist, went on stage at the MTV music awards and did some sort of satanic homage. I knew a producer at MTV who said that wasn't on the agenda, and they were horrified backstage. Chris Rock was master of ceremonies, and like much of the Black community, had spent some time in church. He went to the mic and told the audience of millions *Get your self to church y'all.* It was funny, and it defused the tension. *And*, there was truth in it. A blasphemy had been committed. Go, get clean. MTV's producers thanked him.

Psalm 109 is a curse against a person—a man in this case. Let him be accused and found guilty. Let his days be short, his children orphans, his wife a widow, his family beggars, his property stolen, his parents unforgiven. Let him be an object of horror and blot out mercy not just for him but for the generation that birthed him and the one that follows him. Now that is a *proper* curse. Not just that the skier would fall down and die, but that her children would, her parents would. *And it's in the Bible.* This is all the more confusing since Jesus commands us not to curse. His words:

> You have heard that it was said to those of ancient times, "You shall not murder," and "whoever murders shall be liable to judgment." But I say to you that if you are angry with a brother or sister, you will be liable to judgment, and if you insult a brother or sister, you will be liable to the council, and if you say, "You fool," you will be liable to the hell of fire. (Matt 5:21–22)

Other parts of the New Testament say the same. Irascible old St. Paul agrees: "Bless those who persecute you; bless and do not curse them" (Rom 12:14). St. Peter piles on "Do not repay evil for evil or abuse for abuse, but, on the contrary, repay with a blessing" (1 Pet 3:9). Do you see the pattern? God is not concerned with what you say when you miss a shot on the golf course. God is concerned with what you do when someone *wrongs* you. When someone *properly* curses you. When Christ is on his cross, he absorbs humanity's curses and doles out grace undeserved. We're far past the bedroom or the bathroom here.

When I was a kid on my street, there was a word salad of cusswords that the other kids on my block taught. I still remember it, though I won't repeat it here. But one kid got very grave and said, "Never to say that. It means 'God, go to hell.'" It's the worst thing you can say. He understood words have power. In the South we'll say to someone, "Well, bless your heart." That's a way of suffocating someone with sugar.

More seriously now, Psalm 109 has been used in US political discourse. For years some would "joke" that it was a prayer they could actually pray for President Obama. That his parents be cursed—you know, his African ancestry. Let his children be cursed. This is the worst of religion—using faith to gain power and cloak racism in respectability. It's idolatry, and it's disgusting, and it's getting worse. The real fruit is that it'll keep turning people away from genuine faith. I have sometimes been advised to stop using the word "evangelical." It just means political opportunists, election deniers, those who delegitimize courts and denigrate immigrants. I still love the word. "Evangelical" means gospel people, good news people. And I want our word back. But maybe they're right. I've seen it misused with this psalm. Now, opprobrium is not new in politics. And if you look at how folks spoke of their rivals in the 1800s, it would be worse. It's just we *thought* our age had improved, that we'd moved past racist attacks and denigrating whole swaths of people. Clearly, we have not. We human beings are as rotten as ever. Who will save us from ourselves?

A teacher of mine, a lit professor, saw the whole gospel once . . . in the graffiti on a bathroom stall.[1] It used some genuine curses I won't repeat here. It cursed Black people—different verb, different noun. It cursed White people in return. There you see our culture—five hundred years of Europeans abusing minorities, a few decades of minorities standing up for themselves. Over both slurs, a third person had written "Jesus saves." *That's* who Jesus saves—the ugliest of us; those who curse the worst in the most unclean ways and deserve saving the least. Jesus doesn't save the deserving. No, no, no. They don't need it. Jesus saves the *un*deserving. Now that's a dangerous truth.

It is hard to imagine a psalm that behaves worse than 109. I'm almost hesitant to tell you it's in the Bible. But there's a lot of scripture that curses. And as your preacher I owe you an explanation. Because even if *I* don't tell you such passages are in the Bible, you'll find them. Or politicians will use them, and you won't know how to respond. So, Psalm 109. What's this curse of all curses doing in our Bible?

I taught a class of Jews and Christians with a rabbi colleague in Vancouver. We visited shul together and church together. And wouldn't you know it, in church there was a passage about "the Jews" plotting against Jesus. I'm sitting there with Jewish friends, including a Holocaust survivor. She was *scared*. She leaned over to me, "Jason, there are little kids in here." Afterwards we had a

1. The great Tony Abbot of Davidson College, now of blessed memory.

discussion and she said, "You guys *can't* read passages like that anymore; it's dangerous." And a fellow Jewish student said, "Well, hold on a minute. In *our* Bible we also have curses. And we also have no way to take passages out. *Every* passage has been used for harm." My rabbi colleague said, "You know, right after the Exodus, when God destroys slavery, there are laws about how to treat slaves. I would never want a guest to think we Jews support slavery, but it's there." I told her later, "Wow, Rabbi, you really saved my bacon, thank you." She said "Don't ever say that to a Jewish person again, OK?"

Well, why is Psalm 109 cursing this poor man? What did he ever do?

> 16 He did not remember to show kindness
> but pursued the poor and needy
> 17 He loved to curse; let curses come on him.

He mistreated the poor, and he cursed others. In a way, this is a prayer for karma. Let what goes around come around. If someone is bad to the poor and curses others, let that boomerang back around on them. If there's a central claim about God in the Bible it's this: God loves the poor. *Loves* them. If you ever, like me, find yourself tempted to curse the poor—"Man, get a job. Get your act together. I'm not giving to you; you'll just drink the money"—think again. Words have power. And curses can boomerang. Instead, say a word of blessing.

A friend of mine likes to wander around cemeteries. I do too. They're fascinating. We both have shrinks working overtime. He found a rough stone once from a previous century that said this: "She had her faults, but she was good to the poor." Who felt the need to put the first part?! "She had her faults." But the second part—"she was good to the poor"—that's worth being buried under, isn't it?

But surely being bad to the poor is not enough to be cursed for generations—someone's children, someone's parents. Something more is going on here. The psalmist is in real trouble.

> 26 Help me, O LORD my God!

Let my assailants be put to shame,
29 May my accusers be clothed with dishonor;
may they be wrapped in their own shame as in a mantle.

This is mortal danger. Trapped with no way out. "God, what they mean for me, do that to them and more." You've heard of the Old Testament command "an eye for an eye" (Exod 21:24). Sounds harsh. Gandhi famously said, "an eye for an eye makes the whole world blind." But the command is actually there to *limit* violence. If someone does harm to you, you can only do the same amount of harm back, no more. If someone takes your eye, you can't take both of theirs. It's actually the beginning of a system of laws instead of mob justice. The one praying is in trouble and doesn't deserve it—let that same trouble be doled out to those who make it.

Dietrich Bonhoeffer, the great German pastor and theologian who resisted the Nazis, says there are some psalms *only* Jesus can pray.[2] Psalms that say "I am entirely innocent." That's true of Jesus Christ alone, none of the rest of us. Psalms that say "Everyone is against me." We may *feel* that way sometimes. But Jesus Christ is the true man of sorrows, the one all humanity lines up against and curses.

If *I* had a giant red button with which to blow up the world, I'd use it several times a day. I don't know how presidents do it with that nuclear football following them at all times. But of course they'd blow themselves up too if they used it, and everyone they love. The only one righteous enough to condemn all others is Jesus Christ. And what does he do? *Saves* others. Saves us. We who condemned him and deserve only condemnation.

What if Jesus is the cursed man in this psalm? He's the one *we* rise up against in accusation. There is an accuser on his right—the other crucified man. Jesus is tried and found guilty. *His* days are few. He *has* no wife or children, no human father either, in fact. He has no property. Crucifixion is how Romans erased human beings. Tens of thousands of slaves they crucified, and we know the name

2. Dietrich Bonhoeffer, *Life Together/Prayer Book of the Bible*, trans. G. L. Müller and A. Schönherr, Dietrich Bonhoeffer Works 5 (Minneapolis: Fortress, 1995).

of one: Jesus of Nazareth. Purported king of the Jews. The rest are accursed from history and blotted out from the record. We human beings curse God in the flesh and crucify Jesus. *We* say "God, go to hell." And you know what? He does—as we confess in the Creed and see in Orthodox icons of Easter. And he saves everybody in the place. Iconographers show this by depicting him lifting out Adam and Eve. We have no curse he can't turn around for blessing.

All of our curses fall on the man on the cross. And what does he give us back? Mercy. He forgives his executioners, his betraying friends, his weak fellow human beings. He comes back not with vengeance but with restoration. "Here, see my wounds; this blood means life forever, drink up."[3] And this is key: He enables us to do as he does. To receive curses and give back nothing but blessings. St. Paul puts it this way: "Christ redeemed us . . . by becoming a curse for us—for it is written, 'Cursed is everyone who hangs on a tree,' in order that in Christ Jesus the blessing of Abraham might come to the gentiles" (Gal 3:13). Christ *becomes* a curse, to leach all of humanity's poison out of us and transfigure us all into blessing.

So friends, please never think the church is there to make us avoid using naughty words. Such a small prize, not worth the effort. Here's what the church *is* there for. To gather all of us who curse God. And to say: This God whom you curse, he is risen from the grave we put him in, and all he does is bless you, and everyone else—especially the others you'd rather curse. Thanks be to God. Amen.

3. I know it's audacious and dangerous to paraphrase God. But it's not less audacious or dangerous to preach in the first place.

CHAPTER V

Psalm 149

Boo, other nations!

Jason Byassee

Psalm 149

1 Praise the LORD!
Sing to the LORD a new song,
his praise in the assembly of the faithful.
2 Let Israel be glad in its Maker;
let the children of Zion rejoice in their King.
3 Let them praise his name with dancing,
making melody to him with tambourine and lyre.
4 For the LORD takes pleasure in his people;
he adorns the humble with victory.
5 Let the faithful exult in glory;
let them sing for joy on their couches.
6 Let the high praises of God be in their throats
and two-edged swords in their hands,
7 to execute vengeance on the nations
and punishment on the peoples,
8 to bind their kings with fetters
and their nobles with chains of iron,
9 to execute on them the judgment decreed.
This is glory for all his faithful ones.
Praise the LORD!

When my family crossed the border as we relocated from the US to Canada, I told our eight-year-old that Canada had a queen. As a good American he said, "Aw, that means we're not free."

My favorite bumper sticker about our national identity says this: "Canada, we could have had French food, British culture, and American technology. Instead we have British food, American culture, and French technology." I think it's funny every time. Our problem as Canadians, it seems to me, is our negative definition. The key cultural thing for us Canadians is that we're not Americans. Americans are loud, aggressive, religious, gun-toting, paying for healthcare out of pocket. We're the opposite. Or we'll speak about our vast geographic scope. But most of it's water and farther north than any of us will ever go. Our identity was somewhat clearer when we were what was left of the British Empire in North America. But that was always awkward with our French inheritance and indigenous legacy. The question for us Canadians is this: Who are we, y'all?

We're an absolutely lovely country. I love so much about Canada. You know, things like our national healthcare system, which we're so proud of. I know we underfund it, I know we're confused and confusing about Medical Assistance in Dying, problems abound. We want to pay taxes like Americans but get services like Scandinavians. But try and take province-run healthcare away, and this country would take to the streets. And it all comes from a Baptist youth group. Tommy Douglas was a youth pastor in Saskatchewan who realized his Depression-era kids didn't need a pool table. They needed health care. He got elected to the provincial legislature and got it passed. And all the doctors went on strike. They called it a communist plot. But the people of Saskatchewan said, "Actually, we like it." The rest of the country followed. Canadian healthcare is an important national symbol, as important as the NHS is to our British forebears. And it was born in a Baptist youth ministry. The CBC held an election of sorts for the most beloved Canadian in history. Wayne Gretzky finished tenth. Number one was Baptist minister Tommy Douglas![1]

1. Wikipedia, "The Greatest Canadian," https://en.wikipedia.org/wiki/The_Greatest_Canadian.

I do appreciate our relationship to the British Commonwealth. America's national character was formed over against Britishness with a violent rebellion. You can still see that in my country's MO: Fight first, ask questions later. Canada had a negotiation with the monarch, and we got a country. There's a reason we major in diplomacy—Lester Pearson won our last Nobel Peace Prize for negotiating peace in the Suez Crisis in the '50s. We're a middle-weight power. We can't just throw our weight around. So we talk instead of fight. When Bono said "the world needs more Canada," he meant this tradition. Peace, order, and good government is rather different than life, liberty, and the pursuit of happiness. You probably know that happiness was originally "property" in Thomas Jefferson's early drafts, which in 1776 meant slaves. I'm proud that Ontario was founded as the first province in the British Empire to outlaw slavery, that we were Canaan on the Underground Railroad. Canada is far, far from perfect, we all know. We're trying to figure out how to tell our story vis-à-vis indigenous peoples dispossessed and traumatized. Even there I see the church leading the way. What is an apology but repentance, an effort at right relationships? A friend tells a story of indigenous leaders meeting with ministers and lawyers to pursue an apology from the United Church for our role in the residential schools, which came in 1998. In the meeting one indigenous elder noted, "When it's time to pray, it's either us or the pastors. How about you lawyers?" They all looked at each other. No class on prayer in law school. One finally offered up a "to whom it may concern" sort of prayer. Was he going to refuse the elder's request? Indigenous Canadians are more likely to profess Christian faith now than European ones. As we pursue right relations, we may find Jesus there waiting for us. He does that kind of thing, you know.

Any citizen of any country who is paying attention could complain all day about their country. Here's what the gospel says. Every country falls short. Every one does. There is only one true republic. The city of God. It's a realm ruled by Christ and built on love of God and neighbor. Every other city is built on pride, on violence to protect against the neighbor. Like a lot of post-Christian countries I worry what holds Canada together. The chance to make money? That's what gets people most animated politically. If so, are the poor losers, the middle class also-rans? Christianity says no—judge a country on how we treat our poor. Jesus Christ commands us to visit those in prison. Because he is them, they him. Do we know how our prisoners are treated in Canada? I don't. I know they're disproportionately indigenous. That people with money tend not to land there. But what if God will judge us one day on how we treated our prisoners? If we ask whether our country makes it easier to be good or not, we'll all have much to repent for. Billy Graham said he wished the US would follow Canada in its foreign policy.[2] What it means to be an evangelical like Graham is to repent, beg forgiveness. That's no humiliation. It's the most powerful thing you can ever do.

Psalm 149 belongs on any list of rude psalms. It starts out praising politely enough. Then it turns.

> 6 Let the high praises of God be in their throats
> and two-edged swords in their hands,
> 7 to execute vengeance on the nations
> and punishment on the peoples,
> 8 to bind their kings with fetters
> and their nobles with chains of iron,
> 9 to execute on them the judgment decreed.
> This is glory for all his faithful ones.
> Praise the Lord!

Uh, yeah, praise God, we conquered and killed everybody . . . . The reference is to the conquest of the nations in the promised land. Israel was a nation of slaves, delivered by God's powerful hand from Pharaoh through the Red Sea, then crossing the Jordan into Canaan, it defeated nations there and settled into the land flowing with milk and honey. Beat the Canaanites, the Amalekites, a bunch of other 'ites. Course Israel kept fighting those enemies. It still does. And the milk and honey don't always flow so freely. That's a

2. Grant Wacker, *America's Pastor: Billy Graham and the Shaping of a Nation* (Boston: Belknap, 2014), 230.

glimpse of us: humanity, either fighting with or sleeping with our enemies. A people desperate for mercy.

Whenever there's a US-led war you'll see bumper stickers in Canada, "God bless every nation—no exceptions." A very Canadian thing to say. My native USA likes to speak of itself as a chosen nation on analogy to Israel. That can be a dangerous way to speak—to assume God is on your side and against your enemies. In biblical faith, we say that's idolatry. Bandying God around like a mascot to bless your causes. The true God of Israel often fights *against* Israel. Often gives victory to her enemies, especially when Israel is unfaithful. You sure you want *this* God on your side? God punishes, doesn't just bless. But again maybe that's the problem in the first place. Speaking of God as choosing a side at all. Having a people. Electing Israel. Once you say that, haven't you nearly guaranteed violence? This psalm's near neighbor, Psalm 147, ends this way:

> 19 He declares his word to Jacob,
> his statutes and ordinances to Israel.
> 20 *He has not dealt thus with any other nation;*
> *they do not know his ordinances.*

Really? Does God just curse all the other nations? I notice my Jewish friends get nervous talking about Israel's chosenness. It can sound like others are not-chosen, not-loved by God. They don't mean that at all. But doesn't God taking sides indicate the other side is, lesser? I sometimes tease my fellow Canadians that we know who we are by saying we're better than America. Whatever America is, we're morally superior. That's impressive—we look at the nation we consider the most arrogant nation on earth and we say, "Oh yeah, we're even better!"

Here's how I view Israel's chosenness. At first, God deals with all humanity. Adam and Eve. The only people. Paradise, and just one rule. Of course, we break it and are punished. So God gives a few more rules. Ok, don't murder. And Cain murders Abel. Things go downhill from there. So God says, "Alright, that's enough, I'm wiping everybody out and starting over with the one good family.

Noah's. I'm getting rid of these bad people and doubling down on the only good ones." But ten minutes after the flood, Noah's drunk and cursing his own children forever. Well, that didn't work out. So God tries this. "I'm choosing a family to repair the world. Not the best family. The most unlikely one. Abram and Sarai. No kids. In their nineties. I'm making them leave their homeland to follow me. And through them I'll fill the earth with blessings." I love this: When God wants to repair the world, he doesn't send an army, a general, an empire, a natural disaster. God sends a family. A couple too old to have children whose descendants will repair the world. Genesis puts it this way:

> [1] Now the LORD said to Abram, "Go from your country and your kindred and your father's house to the land that I will show you. [2] I will make of you a great nation, and I will bless you and make your name great, so that you will be a blessing. [3] I will bless those who bless you, and the one who curses you I will curse, and in you all the families of the earth shall be blessed."
>
> [4] So Abram went, as the LORD had told him. (Gen 12:1–4)

God's people Israel. I don't mean the country with the flag, that's one expression of Judaism, I mean all fifteen million Jewish people on the globe.

That promise still stands. God has chosen Israel and can't unchoose them. Eventually God comes among us *as an Israelite*. A Jew. A human. Jesus. To show us all how to live. To die for us. And rise and raise us all. I don't mean God chooses Israel and not Palestine. No—here's the weird way God saves the world. God chooses one people *through whom* to bless all the others. We religious types can get confused and say "God chose us—and not them, hurray!" No, God's blessings aren't *for* us. They're *through* us *for* everybody else. And being chosen can be hard. Ask Israel. It's like being the teacher's pet. The rest of the class resent the teacher's pet. Ask Jesus on his cross. Being chosen means God squeezes blessings out of you for the world: leaves you mangled; others beautified.

Now I hope you get a little nervous when I say God chooses Israel and can't unchoose. Does that cause superiority? Arrogance? The sort of violence we see in Gaza or Ukraine? I don't think so, or at least it doesn't have to. When I quote Bono saying "the world needs more Canada" we Canadians don't want to go invade somebody. We feel proud. "Yeah, you're right, more talking less fighting would be great." When God chooses Israel it's like you or me choosing a spouse. We're not saying all other women or men are bad. No. Just that I'm going to make my life with this one. Bind myself to them and none other. Not because the others are bad. But because this is the one for me. When one of you says your grandchild is the greatest grandchild in world history, I don't think you hate the other children! "Nah, all children are great. But the one with my genes, my kid as their mum, my shared stories. Of course they're my favorite."

When this psalm was first sung, it was looking back on conquering the nations in the promised land, binding kings, executing judgment. But by the time it was written down, centuries later, Judah was in exile. Israel's leaders are in fetters, its nobles bound, judgment executed, the people punished. There barely was an Israel left anymore. No king. No land. No temple. No nothin'. God's promises . . . failed. Israel remembers this time of prosperity from a position of poverty. Hardly a place of superiority or arrogance. On the contrary, she was a nation of convicts, reduced to begging, all proud arrogance lost. And when her last and greatest king comes, he's bound with fetters. He wears a crown of thorns. His throne is a cross from which he rules the world. There is no place for national or ethnic arrogance in Christian faith. It is a faith of humility, of a cross, of a servant who washes our feet and commands us to love enemies. Friedrich Nietzsche, our most interesting atheist, hated Christianity because we exalt weakness. He wanted people to be strong, great, to throw off servanthood and step into power. The Nazis followed his lead. Some of my fellow Americans love this language of seeking greatness, all others be damned. But we Christians see God *only* in humility, service, self-emptying. I agree the world needs more Canada. But what it really needs more of is Jesus.

You know how every American who comes north to speak or perform compliments Canada? Often they'll say, if things keep going the way they are, moving to Canada sounds pretty good. Like after a ham-fisted political move by the US or a disastrous election. Mine is one American family that did make this move. Let me tell you, it's not so easy. I've met people who came to the Canadian border in the '60s and were just waived in: "You're against the Vietnam War? So are we! Come on in! Here's some maple syrup!" But now you have to get permits and prove you're not taking someone's job and take tests and spend tens of thousands. I've written or edited twenty books, and my written English test was the lowest grade I got on citizenship exams. Whatever. Anyway, one American friend named Eugene Cho preached at the church I was involved with in Vancouver. Said he wished he could move to Canada then, in 2018. He had been a great church planter in Seattle, now he works in Washington, DC for a hunger advocacy organization called Bread for the World. But when he first came to America, he felt he was a failure. His siblings, good Korean kids, were a doctor and a lawyer. Instead of becoming an engineer, he disappointed his parents—became a pastor. Grrrr. No money in it. But he impressed them by going to Princeton Seminary. Moved to California to plant a church. And . . . it flopped. His mom came to visit him and he got up early, 5 a.m., to sneak out to his job at Barnes & Noble, and she was already up praying for him. "Why are you up, son?" "Mom, I failed, lost my job, I'm a janitor at a bookstore." Now, that's nothing to be ashamed of. But in an immigrant family that moved for professional opportunity, he felt so much shame. She got up from her prayers. Walked over to him. Was she going to hit him? Say she was ashamed? No. She got her coat. And said, "Come on, I'll go clean the store with you, we'll get done twice as fast together." Her faith overcame her desire for greatness for her kid. Her prayers reminded her that real greatness is service. And he felt loved. When Donald Trump attacked Asian people for causing COVID, Eugene took up their defense.[3] On behalf of the Asian-American community he resisted racism and demonstrated Jesus' way in a country more taken with Nietzsche's ways of power and greatness. I'd say he made good after all, wouldn't you? Eugene, don't stay in Canada. America needs you.

My favorite Canadian success stories are of our welcome of immigrants. The US used to be proud of welcoming new people; now our doors are closed apparently. The debate is whether to be awful to immigrants or whether to be even more awful. We Canadians have a history of Ukrainian immigrants moving here after the war. One such family was called Gretzky. We wouldn't have had the Great One, the most Canadian of hockey dads or his son #99, without immigration. Our most vibrant and fastest-growing Christian communities in Canada are Filipino, Chinese, Iranian—they're even more likely to embrace faith here, statistically, than they were back home. When I lived in Vancouver I heard about the Hungarian uprising in 1956 against the communists. My friend, a professor there, got a phone call from UBC's president. "Hey, you know German, right?" "Yeah." "That's like Hungarian, right?" "No, not at all!" "Whatever. A whole forestry department just snuck over the border into Austria with their families. And I just gave 'em all jobs." "Sir, we already have a forestry department." "Yeah, now we got two. Can you go take 'em around to get bank accounts, get their kids settled in school?" My friend went on to welcome immigrants the rest of his life. I hear stories of this church mobilizing in the '70s to receive Vietnamese refugees, in the last few years to receive Syrian ones. God bless you. When a friend of mine at UBC tried to revive the hospitality to the Hungarians in the '50s by welcoming Syrians, he got no response. They're in danger! "But they're Muslims. How do we know they're safe?" We don't! Nothing is safe! Doing nothing isn't safe either! And real greatness is hospitality to those in danger.

Here's an early church description of Christians and citizenship:

3. Sarah Pulliam Bailey, "Evangelical Leader Denounces Trump for Calling Coronavirus 'the Chinese virus,'" *Washington Post*, March 17, 2020.

> Christians are indistinguishable from other people either by nationality, language, or customs. They do not inhabit separate cities of their own, or speak a strange dialect, or follow some outlandish way of life. . . . With regard to dress, food, and manner of life in general, they follow the customs of whatever city they happen to be living in, whether it is Greek or foreign.
>
> And yet there is something extraordinary about their lives. They live in their own countries as though they were only passing through. They play their full role as citizens, but labor under all the disabilities of aliens. Any country can be their homeland, but for them their homeland, wherever it may be, is a foreign country. Like others, they marry and have children, but they do not abandon them. They share their meals, but not their wives
>
> They pass their days upon earth, but they are citizens of heaven.[4]

It's not surprising our country falls short. Every one does. Even the best country is a pale imitation of the city of God, the kingdom Christ is bringing, one where the poor are blessed, the arrogant humbled, where we're all transfigured into Jesus' likeness. Until Jesus comes back and brings his kingdom, I'm happy to celebrate Canada Day with perogies and a beaver tail. Let's all give thanks for a kingdom and a king who accept everyone, especially the ones no one else wants, with the words "welcome home." Amen.

4. *Letter to Diognetus* 5, https://www.vatican.va/spirit/documents/spirit_20010522_diogneto_en.html.

CHAPTER VI

Psalm 137

Bashing baby brains

Jason Byassee

1 By the rivers of Babylon—
there we sat down, and there we wept
when we remembered Zion.
2 On the willows there
we hung up our harps.
3 For there our captors
asked us for songs,
and our tormenters asked for mirth, saying,
"Sing us one of the songs of Zion!"
4 How could we sing the LORD's song
in a foreign land?
5 If I forget you, O Jerusalem,
let my right hand wither!
6 Let my tongue cling to the roof of my
mouth,
if I do not remember you,
if I do not set Jerusalem
above my highest joy.
7 Remember, O LORD, against the Edomites
the day of Jerusalem's fall,
how they said "Tear it down! Tear it down!

Down to its foundations!"
8 O daughter Babylon, you devastator!
Happy shall they be who pay you back
what you have done to us!
9 Happy shall they be who take your little ones
and dash them against the rock!

Recently something happened that's never happened to me before. Someone new told me they came to church . . . because of the sermon title. They'd seen it on the sign out there, "Boo, other nations," for Canada Day. I don't love titling sermons. Half the time I dream up a title way in advance, and by the time that Sunday rolls around I forget why I chose it. But that day I did talk about the rude psalms that condemn other nations, as promised on the sign.

This reflection is a good deal *more* sensationalist: bashing baby brains.[1] If someone turns up for a sermon title like that, may be best not to tell me. My titles are sort of the equivalent of headlines in yellow journalism in the nineteenth century, or tabloids in our day. Prurience sells. But with these titles, I haven't doctored the Bible at all. I'm just telling you what it says . . . .

8 O daughter Babylon, you devastator!
Happy shall they be who pay you back
what you have done to us!
9 Happy shall they be who take your little ones
and dash them against the rock!

Infanticide is how you eliminate another people. The psalm offers it as a benediction: "Blessed are those" makes us think of Jesus' Sermon on the Mount. "Blessed are the poor in spirit, for theirs is the kingdom of heaven," for example (Matt 5:3). The language in Psalm 137 is the same. "Blessed" shall they be who take your little ones and dash them. This isn't one of those cases where the Hebrew original or some other manuscript can rescue the verse. It's as awful as it sounds.

So it's perfect for this series on Rude Praise. In most of these sermons I've suggested the psalm offers some fiber to the diet of

1. In fact, we had someone phone the church in outrage after they had driven by and seen the sign with the title. Don't blame me, man, blame God . . . .

our prayers. Good for the whole system. Not here. I don't want us praying these lines. I don't want *anyone* praying these lines. A monastery I visited knew what to do with lines like these. Monks pray the psalms *for a living*. Seven times a day they're in church chanting psalms. Lots of older monks know all 150 by heart. As they used to say in the ancient church, "they know the whole David." People who love the psalms enough to give up money, sex, and power for them . . . *don't say these lines*. They just politely ignore them, and move to the next verse.

So why are they there? And what do we do with them?

The *rest* of psalm 137 is *gorgeous*. It's inspired centuries of composers to do their best work. Some of the rude psalms in this series, Elaine has no music for. This one she could keep us here a long while and not repeat. It has shown up in reggae versions, Sinead O'Connor covered it, Matisyahu has a rap track on it. You can see why.

> 1 By the rivers of Babylon—
> there we sat down, and there we wept
> when we remembered Zion. . . .
> 5 If I forget you, O Jerusalem,
> let my right hand wither!
> 6 Let my tongue cling to the roof of my mouth,
> if I do not remember you,
> if I do not set Jerusalem
> above my highest joy.

It's a rare psalm we can geo-locate—in what we now call Iraq—and date—after 586 BC. The southern tribes of Judah were conquered that year, the people carried off in exile, the temple burnt, their babies murdered. Without the promised land, the temple for worship, the people secure, what is the singer supposed to sing about? Israel *has* songs for Jerusalem, but not Babylon. She has songs for the River Jordan but not for the River Tigris or Euphrates. So the harp is hung up. No more songs.

One way the Nazis dehumanized Jews was to *make* them sing and dance. "Sing for us one of the songs of Zion!" No need to think of a response. There was one right here in the psalm: "How can we sing the Lord's song in a foreign land?"

Scholars call these lament psalms. They dump out sorrow before God. *That's* what I want in our prayers—more tears, more sighing, more longing for the redemption of Jerusalem. But scholars also call these two final verses "imprecatory." Scholars need something to do. It just means cursing. You and I follow Jesus. And he *commands* us not to curse, even enemies (Luke 6:28). That's why the monks won't sing these imprecatory verses. Not because the verses are not nice. But because Jesus tells us not to curse.

Now, curses *can* have their uses. True, Jesus is commanding us not to curse. That's easy enough for him to say—he didn't have to drive around Toronto. More seriously now, I was in the Netherlands last month, and its Reformed churches have a tradition of singing psalms, including 137th. They were occupied for four brutal years by the Nazis. Friends of mine *remember* family being murdered. So the church in the Netherlands would pray these psalms of imprecation.[2] Happy shall they be who do the same to you! Wait, are you resisting the Reich? Oh no, we're just praying these psalms from the Bible. The Dutch under occupation learned what the African-American church long knew: You can code-switch, and your enslavers won't know. "Yeah, these spirituals about Pharaoh and Moses, they're just Bible songs"—about a God who frees slaves and hates tyranny.

A few weeks back, we had an important event in our church about anti-Semitism. We had some nine hundred people register, so many we had to cut it off for fire-code reasons. When do you ever have to turn people away from church because it's full? I told the organizers, "I can't fill the building on Sunday to talk about Jesus, if you guys can on a Monday night *at the same time as game 7 of the Stanley Cup finals*, maybe we should just give y'all the keys." You *think* I'm joking . . . . I met half a dozen Holocaust survivors that night. Two older ladies who'd been hidden in monasteries as little girls. One man hidden on a farm as a boy. A fourth older

2. Martin Tel, "Necessary Songs: The Case for Singing the Entire Psalter," *Christian Century*, January 8, 2014.

woman hidden in a Catholic church. Several have tattoos on their arms from the camps they survived. Our pews feel holier for their having sat on them. Makes you wonder: Would we have the courage to risk hiding those in danger? There was a war on. Not enough food for your own family. And the gestapo searching houses every day. Toni Morrison, the great novelist and essayist and poet, wrote of her fear as an African-American woman that if the trains came for Black people, most of her American neighbors would do nothing. Or would join in loading them. Lots of Nazis saw themselves as doing God's work.

You see what I'm saying? Quoting the Bible is not simple. You can't just say "the Bible says it, I believe it, that settles it." Not every verse has equal weight or stature. And some verses, like this one, read by itself, is a moral horror. The Bible has been used to justify slavery, genocide, dispossession of native peoples, and misogyny. Nearly any moral outrage in church history, there was chapter and verse to support it.

So does this render the Bible useless, or morally suspect? I'm a *preacher* over a Bible in a church, you won't be surprised to know I don't think so. *It's* not morally suspect, *we* are.

Here's what the psalm teaches us. First, life was *hard*! You and I expect to live long and comfortable and pain-free lives. Not so in ancient Israel or most places today. The great preacher Charles Spurgeon said this to his congregation in Victorian London:

> Let those who find fault with it who have never seen their temple burned, their city ruined, their wives ravished, and their children slain; they might not, perhaps, be quite so velvet-mouthed if they had suffered after this fashion.[3]

Of course, almost any atrocity is preceded by its perpetrator claiming to be a victim. Even the Nazis felt the need to pretend they weren't aggressors—yeah, the Poles started this, or it's the Jews' fault. When Jesus commands us to respond to evil with

3. Charles Spurgeon, *The Treasury of David* (Grand Rapids: Kregel, 1976), 627.

good, to turn the other cheek, not to seek revenge, he's speaking *to oppressed people*, crushed by Roman occupation and desperate poverty.[4] The Jews in the Bible *had* been mistreated by the Babylonians, but of course that doesn't give them license to mistreat others. You might notice there's a side glance at the Edomites. These are Israel's neighbors, frenemies: sometime friends, sometime enemies. It seems that the Israelites asked for help and didn't get it. Instead, they got mockery, an anchor thrown to a drowning person. And you may remember the Edomites are descended from Esau, Jacob's twin brother. This psalm is partly a *family* feud: at your *worst* moment, your sibling, your twin, says, "Got what you deserved, didn't you? About time."

Israel shows who we are as human beings. *We* keep record of wrongs, unlike God. We want revenge, not reconciliation. I don't know about you, but my mind does keep a list of who I think has what coming to them. The great Frederick Buechner wrote this:

> Of the Seven Deadly Sins, anger is possibly the most fun. To lick your wounds, to smack your lips over grievances long past, to roll over your tongue the prospect of bitter confrontations still to come, to savor to the last toothsome morsel both the pain you are given and the pain you are giving back—in many ways it is a feast fit for a king. The chief drawback is that what you are wolfing down is yourself. The skeleton at the feast is you.[5]

Or as they say in the recovery community, bitterness is drinking poison and hoping the other person dies.

So Israel is in a rage. Who can blame them? But as a preacher friend of mine says, not everything depicted in the Bible is commended.[6] This sort of curse is meant to horrify us. But there are times to pray with rage. This is a way to pray against cancer, for

4. Miroslav Volf, *Exclusion and Embrace: Theological Exploration of Identity, Otherness, and Reconciliation* (Nashville: Abingdon, 1994), 100.

5. Frederick Buechner *Wishful Thinking: A Theological A B C* (San Francisco: Harper & Row, 1973), 2.

6. My ministry colleague David Larmour of King Street Community Church in Oshawa, ON.

example. Let those new little cells not grow or metastasize. Let them be strangled in the crib. Folks who struggle with addiction—to substances or gambling or porn or shopping—tell me the desires start out small, but then they grow overwhelming. *When* they're small, drown them in the tub. The great C. S. Lewis thinks of the whiny voice that seeks recognition, and fumes when others get it: "Knock the little babies' brains out," he says.[7]

You see what I'm doing here? I'm taking these words seriously *by* applying them spiritually. This is no call to harm anyone's human child. God doesn't want that, we know full well from the rest of the Bible. Anyone with a *conscience* knows that. So these Babylonian babies are metaphorical. They are the worst things *in ourselves*: Envy. Lust. Pride. Don't let them grow up into adult vices.

Another go. In 1 Corinthians 10:4, Paul identifies the rock in the wilderness, from which our ancestors in Israel drank, with Jesus Christ. *He's* the rock to build our house. Our hymns speak often of Christ as our rock. So what would it mean to dash enemy infants against *him*? Take every idea, every thought, just born, and hurl it straight to Jesus. In our language we also speak derogatorily of infants at times. "Don't be a baby" is not something we say to *actual* babies. Take any thought and hurl it to Jesus as fast as possible. When you're tempted to curse that other driver, dash them against Jesus instead.

I know there's something deep in us Protestants that doesn't trust non-literal readings of the Bible. Catholics do sacraments, we do scripture. But bear with me. We read creatively in other parts of our lives. Lovers do it as they reread letters over and over, looking for clues beneath the surface. Spies write texts that misdirect on purpose, with a decoder on the other end. Fiction authors *also* misdirect on purpose. It's more fun. The Bible is at least as sophisticated as a love letter, a code, a novel. Psalm 137 speaks of Jerusalem. This verse is on the sign outside now: "If I forget you, oh Jerusalem, may my right hand wither." But what *is* Jerusalem? It's a city. You can go there. It has postal codes and a mayor and traffic.

7. C. S. Lewis, *Reflections on the Psalms* (New York: Harcourt, 1958), 136.

But poets always make Jerusalem bigger than even that great city. It's a symbol for all of Israel. For all humanity. Sometimes called Zion in the Psalms, it's an image for *the church*; the whole people of God. It's an image for *righteousness*; Jerusalem the *holy* city. It's an image for *heaven*; the city of God come down to us, adorned like a bride processing up that center aisle. Don't ask which reading is right or wrong. They can *all* be right. Now look, there are some simple texts you want more precise: IKEA instructions; parking rules; doctors' prescriptions. Minimal creativity, please. But those aren't the texts that set souls on fire.

When I say "the River Jordan," you don't first think of the actual waterway. You think of death, as the African-American church taught us. Or of baptism. Or of the promised land. When Barack Obama was elected president, Jesse Jackson said, "Today we crossed the river."[8]

Once when I was in literal Jerusalem, I couldn't sleep and found myself walking around the wall of the old city. I thought, ok, why not walk around the whole city? When else am I gonna do that? I turned and saw the street go sharply down. And get dark. Uh, not doing that. Then I laughed out loud. Of course. Zion is on a mountain. You go *up* to Zion. Literally and figurally. I'm not walking down there—that's where *Gehenna* is—hell, or where you get mugged. Can you feel the metaphor coming?

This is how language always works; on multiple levels. But on every level, God loves us, and all humanity, and wants full life for every creature. Read the individual bits in light of that great truth.

Some say that cursing out loud against Edomites and Babylonian children is a sort of therapy. These denunciations are vocalized, so that they're *not* acted upon. Like how therapists will have you say stuff to them you wish you could say to the person who hurt you. I'm not so sure. Most real-world violence starts with words. Before Jews were targeted with bullets they were targeted with words. Before Hutus in Rwanda went after Tutsis with clubs they went after them with slurs. Anti-gay words bring anti-gay violence. I can see validity in leaching poison

8. I borrow this story, with thanks, from David McAllister-Wilson.

out of us so we don't spray it on others. But it's not my preferred reading. See, when you allow multiple readings, it doesn't mean anything goes. The community together decides: "Nah, that one doesn't work." But *how* do we decide?

The best solution comes from St. Augustine, a fourth/fifth-century African church father.[9] Augustine said this: Read every text in the Bible in such a way that your interpretation builds the community's love of God and neighbor. If you interpret a scripture and your hearers don't love their neighbor more, start over. You did it wrong. Because that's what the Bible is *for*. To change us from selfish creatures into saints. If we read the Bible in a way that makes us say, "There, see that? It shows you're bad, and I've been right all along!" . . . No, you just turned that book into poison. But if we read it and repent of our *own* sins, good. We're starting to make progress.

And where does St. Augustine get this rule? From one Jesus of Nazareth (Luke 18:18–20). A lawyer comes to him. Alert: Jesus dislikes lawyers almost as much as he dislikes religious leaders. Lawyer asks: "What do I need for eternal life?" Jesus gives us the golden rule: "Love the Lord your God," and "love your neighbor as yourself." The first part is from Deuteronomy, the second from Leviticus, close to our Jewish elder siblings' hearts as well. In Judaism, they sometimes speak of a silver rule, articulated by Rabbi Hillel, around the time of Jesus: "Whatever is hateful to you: don't do that to your neighbor. All the rest is just commentary." I wonder who's going to grab for a diamond rule . . . .

Rabbis Jesus and Hillel knew there *are* things worth raging against. We pray about most of them every week. Israel and Gaza. Ukraine and Russia. Uighurs in camps in China. Homelessness and hunger in wealthy Toronto. Our own self-destructiveness. Let's maybe try a bold step further and pray

9. Augustine, *On Christian Teaching*, translated by R. P. H. Green (New York: Oxford, 2008), 27.

this verse out loud. I respect my monk friends deeply, but let's try something different. And then notice what happens when we curse our enemies. Our curses . . . fall on Jesus. They land like nails in his hands; thorns on his brow; a cross on his back. Christ does leach all our poison out . . . and then he drinks it. And gives us back life, blessings—we who curse. Do you see? All Christ does with our curses is transfigure them into blessings.

I'll conclude with a story that shocked me like this psalm shocks all of us. A young friend of mine is one of the best United Church ministers we have. He wears his clerical collar around on transit—because he's braver than I am. A few weeks ago on the TTC someone came up to him and said, "You're no priest" and spat in his face. No idea why. Maybe there's place for such rage—maybe someone else in a clerical collar harmed the spitter. That doesn't make it ok. My friend is gay, not too outwardly, but maybe that's what drew the ire. That would make it worse. Whatever it is, it's awful. But all I could think of was Jesus, also spat upon, despised. And he absorbed all that rejection and made from it acceptance for *us* who spit on him. Jesus says

> Blessed are you when people revile you and persecute you and utter all kinds of evil against you falsely on my account. Rejoice and be glad, for your reward is great in heaven. (Matt 5:11)

Hey—no one said being a Christian would be easy. Just that it's the way to life.

CHAPTER VII

Psalm 88

The Bible's only tragic ending

Jason Byassee

Psalm 88

1 O LORD, God of my salvation,
at night, when I cry out before you,
2 let my prayer come before you;
incline your ear to my cry.
3 For my soul is full of troubles,
and my life draws near to Sheol.
4 I am counted among those who go down to the Pit;
I am like those who have no help.
5 like those forsaken among the dead,
like the slain that lie in the grave,
like those whom you remember no more,
for they are cut off from your hand.
6 You have put me in the depths of the Pit,
in the regions dark and deep.
7 Your wrath lies heavy upon me,
and you overwhelm me with all your waves. *Selah*
8 You have caused my companions to shun me;
you have made me a thing of horror to them.
I am shut in so that I cannot escape;

> [9] my eye grows dim through sorrow.
> Every day I call on you, O LORD;
> I spread out my hands to you.
> [10] Do you work wonders for the dead?
> Do the shades rise up to praise you? *Selah*
> [11] Is your steadfast love declared in the grave
> or your faithfulness in Abaddon?
> [12] Are your wonders known in the darkness
> or your saving help in the land of forgetfulness?
> [13] But I, O LORD, cry out to you;
> in the morning my prayer comes before you.
> [14] O LORD, why do you cast me off?
> Why do you hide your face from me?
> [15] Wretched and close to death from my youth up,
> I suffer your terrors; I am desperate.
> [16] Your wrath has swept over me;
> your dread assaults destroy me.
> [17] They surround me like a flood all day long;
> from all sides they close in on me.
> [18] You have caused friend and neighbor to shun me;
> my companions are in darkness.

WELL THAT WAS A dismal psalm wasn't it?! It's even sadder than it sounded. The last line in our translation is "my companions are in darkness," a reasonable rendering of the Hebrew. But here's a better one: "Darkness is my only friend."

The psalms are the hymnal of Israel. They are the songs God gives us to teach us how to sing. We have favorite psalms in the church: "The LORD is my shepherd," or "I lift up mine eyes up to the hills." We put those in needlepoint or on cat posters. And then there are psalms like this one today:

> [8] You have caused my companions to shun me;
> you have made me a thing of horror to them.
> I am shut in so that I cannot escape.

Can you feel the claustrophobia? The problem is not just the misery. It's that *God* has brought the misery about: "*You have caused*." I am alone, Lord, and you are to blame. Hard to put that on a throw pillow or send it with an emoji (praying hands!).

We're in a series on rude praise, about psalms that misbehave. This is my last crack at y'all in this series. After today we have excellent guest preachers—some of the best in the world. I'm here a lot but not preaching. I've described this series and several of our guests have said, "Ooh, I like it, *I'll* preach on that too." I think we like it because so much faith comes off as a hallmark card, a fortune cookie, a you-can-do-it sort of pick-me-up. That won't cut it in real life. The Bible is actually a jolt to our superficial religion. It says, "Everything you think is wrong. God and the world are entirely different than you thought." And that's good news. I hear about folks' atheism, and when I ask them to describe the God they don't believe in, I can usually say "I wouldn't believe in that God either."

For example, Psalm 88 has a depth of sorrow that's hard to believe. No matter how crushed you are, this psalm is just as desperate, right there with you.

> I am like those who have no help. (v. 4)
>
> O Lord, why do you cast me off? (v. 14)
>
> Your dread assaults destroy me. (v. 16)

Psalms often bend down to this depth of sorrow. Because we live at this depth. Where everything is broken, and we are abandoned by everyone. But biblical psalms usually don't stay there. They bend down, down, down, but then by the end of the psalm they bounce back up to a place of praise and gratitude.

Jesus on his cross does a good Jewish thing: he quotes a psalm. No need to make up a prayer, God has already given us one. "My God, my God, why have you forsaken me?" Theologians have been kept *very* busy trying to understand how the second person of the Trinity could be abandoned by the first. But by the end of Psalm 22, all is right with the world again:

> 25 From you comes my praise in the great congregation;
> my vows I will pay before those who fear him.
> 26 The poor shall eat and be satisfied;
> those who seek him shall praise the Lord.
> May your hearts live forever!

> [27] All the ends of the earth shall remember
> and turn to the LORD,
> and all the families of the nations
> shall worship before him.
> [28] For dominion belongs to the LORD,
> and he rules over the nations.

From the suffering of one Jew, to worldwide praise from all families of the earth. That's the whole story of the church: Jesus is crushed, and all peoples are blessed. That's a reason to say hallelujah. And that's the shape of most psalms, most of the Bible: from misery to glory.

Not Psalm 88. This one stays in misery. It doesn't bounce back up to glory. It's the Bible's only tragic ending. A Scottish musician I admire named John Bell set this psalm to music, and the conclusion is discordant. And he wrote in a little note to his fellow musicians: *This is not a mistake. It ends as the 88th psalm does.* Don't make it pretty. Leave the psalm jarringly ugly.

And this is such good news. The Bible doesn't always have a happy ending. It can end in sorrow. Because that's where lots of us spend our lives: drowned in sorrow. Wherever you are friends, however deep your sadness, there is another who dives down there with you: God almighty. God's presence is not just for winners, the victorious, the happy. Its for his creatures who suffer the most.

Someone wise points out that our theater in North America tends to love musicals that always end cheerfully. Historians will look back on our day and wonder, "Hmmm, how come these folks were trying so hard to cheer themselves up?" Find me a tragedy on stage or screen. We're nearly pathological about our happy endings. Meanwhile our Greek ancestors *loved* tragedy. It wasn't a good play unless it left you in tears. The Bible is also a tragedy: Everything is ruined. It is a comedy too: Christ's resurrection heals creation. It's even a fairy tale: Your wildest dreams aren't wild enough. But first, tragedy.[1]

1. The language of comedy, tragedy, and fairy tale I take from Frederick Buechner, *Telling the Truth* (San Francisco: HarperOne 2009).

A friend wrote a memoir about her struggles with mental illness, bipolar disorder specifically. She has found health with lots of support and medication and therapy. But she named her book after this psalm's ending: *Darkness Is My Only Companion*.[2] That's how she felt at her lowest, for years. And *that's* where she found God.

There's a reason we say in our creeds that Christ descends into hell. It sounds jarring, discordant too. Him, of all people; there, of all places; doing what? He's descending as low as his most hurting creatures. I sometimes pray with despair. Oh no. That's not getting better. Ay, I have no idea what an *answered* prayer here would even look like. Thing is, I don't have to instruct God how to answer prayer. Whatever hell I think of, Christ is already there, and he's all the healing there is.

But wait, see, there I am making things better, happier again. This psalm is in the Bible *for a reason*. It says, "You don't have to do that. Don't tidy things up. Let them be as bleak as they are."

The great Canadian writer Kate Bowler found that when people spoke to her of her stage-4 cancer in her thirties, they felt the need to end with "at least."[3] "Well, at least you're young." "At least you have your son, your husband." "At least you're . . . at a world-class hospital." At least, at least, at least. Made things worse. Yeah, a son who'll grow up without me. A husband I'm making a widower. A world-class hospital that's no match for incurable cancer. She realized when we say "at least," we're comforting *ourselves*. It's no comfort to the sufferer. Trust her. She searched every dark corner looking for light and found none. So what do we say instead? You can say "I'm so sorry." Or "Can I do the laundry?" Or even this, try this, you can say, "I love you." This psalm gives us permission to let the darkness be dark. Name it. And then go get the person's favorite coffee and sit in the darkness with them. Don't have to say a thing.

2. Kathryn Greene-McCreight, *Darkness Is My Only Companion* (Grand Rapids: Brazos, 2015).

3. Kate Bowler, *Everything Happens for a Reason and Other Lies I Have Loved* (New York: Random House, 2019).

I turned fifty years old recently. It's a good bet half of my life is behind me, maybe two thirds, or a lot more. Friend told me fifty-five is the golden mean. Because you're not stupid anymore, and your body still mostly works. So I got that to look forward to. My wife, Jaylynn, is already fifty-five. She's perfect. I'm at an age when lots of my friends are aging out of their careers *in*voluntarily. I worked in the humanities in academia. Tenure is scarce. What do you do when your career goes away? Everything you ever worked for is gone. Or get blindsided by an illness no one can prepare for. Or another kind of thief in the night: bankruptcy; infidelity; rejection by family. I'm really tempted to tell 'em "at least." "Well, at least, you, uh, have great kids!" *Don't.* Instead you can name the sorrow. You can linger there. No need to pretend. I remember the hardest time in my own life, career going nowhere, misery with my mom. I felt like I wanted to dive underwater at the ocean and never come up. It wasn't a death wish, it was just hey, it's dark down there. No one can see me. And that's . . . weirdly peaceful sounding.

Here's the thing. Jesus wouldn't leave me down there. He doesn't leave the psalmist down there. He won't leave anyone down there alone. There is no hell he doesn't liberate. No darkness he doesn't linger in. This is why I love Christian faith. Our savior is tortured *to death.* No one, I mean *no one*, can look at Jesus and say, "You don't know real suffering."

Our Jewish and Muslim siblings disagree politely here. Messiahs don't die. They bring God's rule, by definition. Look out the window at all the sorrow, Jesus of Nazareth must not be Messiah. That's our Jewish friends' polite take. I respect it. Muslims say Jesus Christ is a prophet, so he didn't die on the cross. There was a mix-up, and Simon of Cyrene was crucified instead. You can go see Jesus' grave in Punjab. He died with lots of wives and children in peace like a proper prophet. That's our Muslim friends' take. I respect it. Here's our take: The only God there is suffered our worst sorrow, to heal it. To make it and all things new. That's why we don't have to lie and pretend to be cheerful. We can linger in the darkness. Because *that's* where God lingers. At the end of the day, this psalmist is wrong. Darkness is *not* her only companion. God is there too. Darkness is where we meet God. Darkness might be the only place we meet God.

I was sitting with a parishioner in her sorrow recently. I asked about her friends. She said "I wouldn't be here without my friends. What I'm facing is awful. But with their support, I'm going to make it." That's the greatest wealth in life: friendship. The psalmist doesn't have it. The one praying has been abandoned by friends and is alone: "You have caused friend and neighbor to shun me; darkness is my only friend" (v. 18). There again I want to say: Christ hides in that dark. What we feared as kids is incorrect. The dark is not full of monsters. It's full of Jesus.

I was complaining to a friend once about some sadness, I don't remember which honestly. She heard me out. And she said, "Well, I once would have said, 'Lucky you. God must be bringing something better.' I can't say that now. It's not always true, and it's too cheerful. Then I used to say, 'Well, this isn't God. God only brings good things.' But I can't say that now. Sometimes God brings a cross. So here's what I'll say. 'This is an unwelcome gift. It's not what you or anyone wanted. But God is still in it. Bringing grace through it.'" Whatever ill comes, we can't say God did that. God doesn't ever do evil, ever. But we also can't say God is surprised. Out of control. Powerless. No. We have to figure out how to say, "Ok God, this is my cross. How will you work resurrection, here? Not somewhere else, but in my life? What's this unwelcome gift . . . for?"

Friends, whatever you're facing, and I know some of it is bleak. Whatever you're facing, I can promise you two things. One, it will be more painful than you can bear. I can't say, "Always look on the bright side of life." Nope. I can't say, "Every cloud has a silver lining." Ugh. Those cliches are for bad comedies and fortune cookies. Things might get worse. Shakespeare said, "when sorrows come, they come not single spies, but as battalions."[4] Or to use another cliché, when it rains, it pours. Let's back out of cliché-land, whatever we face will be more painful than we can bear. That's Psalm 88. Darkness is our only companion. But Psalm 88 is not

4. *Hamlet*, 4.5.83–84.

the only psalm. We have 149 others. Here's what the others add to it. The second promise I make to you: Whatever you're facing, it will also be more beautiful than you can ever imagine. The God of resurrection is not defeated by death. And God is not afraid of the dark.

I knew a man I admired profoundly. He was from South Sudan, a place riven by warfare. Bombed by Khartoum, shredded by civil war. And in that place God raised up a saint. Joseph Taban Lasuba was from a small minority tribe in the south. Their rival tribes were stronger, so they had learned how to negotiate. Keep them off balance. When you can't fight you learn other kinds of strategies, like talk, poetry, dance, surprising alliances. He also loved his Muslim neighbors. He said, "We have all been mistreated in South Sudan. My Muslim friends know only how to get angry. As a Christian, I tell them forgiveness is stronger than rage." He was going to do a doctoral degree, lead a seminary in Juba, help build a better country. Then he got cancer and died. That's it. Nothing heroic about it. God, you sent us the right person then struck him down. He should have been Nelson Mandela. Instead, his wife is a young widow and his children bereft. There is no why. There is no "at least." There is just sorrow. A friend said this was her only consolation: If God raised up a life like his, God must be planning a resurrection that much more glorious. Feels like a limp hope. But it might be the strongest hope there is.[5]

5. See Ellen Davis's sermon "In Memory of Joseph Taban Lasuba," in her *Preaching the Luminous Word* (Grand Rapids: Eerdmans, 2016), 130–32.

CHAPTER VIII

Psalm 26

Bless me, Lord. After all, I deserve it

Rev. Dayle Barrett

Psalm 26

Plea for Justice and Declaration of Righteousness

Of David.

[1] Vindicate me, O LORD,
for I have walked in my integrity,
and I have trusted in the LORD without wavering.
[2] Prove me, O LORD, and try me;
test my heart and mind.
[3] For your steadfast love is before my eyes,
and I walk in faithfulness to you.

[4] I do not sit with the worthless,
nor do I consort with hypocrites;
[5] I hate the company of evildoers
and will not sit with the wicked.

[6] I wash my hands in innocence
and go around your altar, O LORD,
[7] singing aloud a song of thanksgiving
and telling all your wondrous deeds.

[8] O LORD, I love the house in which you dwell
and the place where your glory abides.
[9] Do not sweep me away with sinners
nor my life with the bloodthirsty,
[10] those in whose hands are evil devices
and whose right hands are full of bribes.

[11] But as for me, I walk in my integrity;
redeem me and be gracious to me.
[12] My foot stands on level ground;
in the great congregation I will bless the LORD.

Rude praise: all the psalms that people don't really quote, the ones you never see on greetings cards, the ones that people don't even read very often, and definitely the ones that people don't preach on. A bit of a challenge.

I can think of a few rude psalms that I can preach about. But we've already had a psalm of lament, the psalmist shaking his fist at the Lord: "God, you're not doing a particularly good job at being God." We had a psalm that sounded a bit too nationalist or xenophobic for our liberal modern tendencies. We had a psalm that ended tragically and didn't even have something happy to go forward with. We had a psalm that cursed people, saying things as horrible as "blessed is the one who dashes the baby's heads against the rocks."

I thought, which psalm am I going to pick? If you read today's psalm and wondered, "Dayle, why did you pick that one?" Maybe you think it isn't a very rude psalm at all. It doesn't shake its fist at God. It doesn't say anything mean about any other nations. Nobody gets cursed. For all intents and purposes, this psalm sounds quite benign. But maybe if you know a little bit about me, you'll understand why this one sounded difficult.

In between the time when I was really young, beginning in ministry and serving the community, and the time later on when I was pursuing ministry and gaining education and preparing to be part of the United Church of Canada, there was about a seven-year gap where I could best be described as an absolute degenerate.

During my late teens, I suffered a great injustice in my life that made me completely question my faith. And I turned from God. I rebelled against God. Anything you would tell your kids not to do, I made sure that I did it. And I made sure that I did it hard. I spent every single night drinking myself into an ugly stupor. I spent every day putting a cocktail of dangerous chemicals into my body. I peddled those chemicals to other people in my community so that I would have what I wanted. I took advantage of women who were looking for love, in order to satisfy my own fleshly lusts and desires. I was, my friends, objectively a bad person. Until about ten years ago when I met this man called Jesus for myself. It went beyond a mere head knowledge of who he was. I already knew the Sunday school stories. I already knew every single story in the Gospels. I already knew the things that Paul had said and that the prophets had prophesied. But now it was different. Because finally I fell on my knees before my Lord and Savior Jesus Christ and said, "God, have mercy upon me, a sinner." And only because of God's grace and God's mercy do I stand before you today clean and sober and in my right mind, standing behind this pulpit preaching to you the gospel. It's because of nothing that I've done, but because Jesus bore my sin upon the cross and rose upon the third day, conquering death, sin, and the grave.

No, I didn't come here to talk about me, but I had to let you know that, so you'd understand why I had a big problem with this psalm. You see, when I read Psalm 26 after all that, it didn't sound right. It didn't sound like a prayer that *I* could pray. Psalm 26 sounds like a prayer for something, somebody who's done everything right, doesn't it? First of all, who goes to God and says, "Lord, judge me"? But even after that, how can I tell God that I've walked in my integrity when I know how often I've lied? How can I say to God that my feet will not slip when I know how often I've fallen? How can I talk to God about hypocrites and idolatrous mortals and evildoers and the wicked when those are the words that one day described me (vv. 4–5)?

When I read Psalm 26, it sounds like it is saying, "Bless me, Lord. After all, I deserve it." And if there's one thing that I was completely certain of, it's that I *didn't* deserve it. It sounded prideful. It sounded arrogant. It sounded like a rude psalm. In fact, it sounded like the exact kind of prayer that Jesus taught us never to pray.

In Luke chapter 18, Jesus tells this parable to people who trusted in themselves and thought they were righteous (Luke 18:9–14). He says:

> Two men went up to the temple to pray, one a Pharisee and the other a tax collector. The Pharisee stood and prayed thus with himself, "God, I thank you that I am not like other men, extortioners, unjust, adulterers, or even as this tax collector. I fast twice a week. I give tithes of all I possess." The tax collector standing afar off would not so much as raise his eyes to heaven, but beat his breast saying, "God, be merciful to me, a sinner!"

And then Jesus says this:

> I tell you, this man went down to his house justified rather than the other; for everyone who exalts himself will be humbled, and he who humbles himself will be exalted.

Now I look at Psalm 26 and at the Pharisee's prayer, and they look a bit similar, don't they? I mean the psalmist is saying that they'll wash their hands in innocence. They're saying that they've walked in God's truth, that they haven't sat with idolatrous mortals or gone in with hypocrites. They've hated the assembly of evildoers. Surely just like the Pharisee, this psalmist is comparing himself to other people and saying that they are better. But if you want to understand the psalm, my friends, you have to understand what it's for. And we know that the Psalms were kind of like *Voices United*, our United Church hymnal, for the people of Israel. It was their book of prayers and hymns. And every hymn, every prayer had a purpose.

When I found out what this one was for, it was quite interesting. Because far from being a prayer bragging at God for how good the person praying was, this was a prayer for somebody who was seeking re-entry to the sanctuary. It was a prayer for somebody who'd been ousted from the community of faith for one reason or another. Maybe they touched something unclean; ate something unclean; or slept with somebody unclean. There are all sorts of reasons that you could have to distance yourself from the community and stay there for a while until you were ready to come back. The whole point of this prayer was that when you came back, you came back asking God to judge you by the integrity, by the truth, that you bear in your heart. You were casting yourself down upon the loving kindness of God. This wasn't a prayer of a perfect person. This was the prayer of a sinner seeking God's mercy. This was a prayer of repentance. And if I can pray anything, I can pray *that.* But not just me, my friends. This is the prayer that we *all* need to pray. Because the gospel truth that I stand before you to tell you is that Christ came to save sinners, of whom I am chief (1 Tim 1:15). But that doesn't make me the only one.

All of us have sinned and fallen short of the glory of God. None of us can come before God in our own power and say, "God! Bless me because I deserve it." But what we can do, if we believe that Jesus Christ bore our sins upon himself, if we believe that he rose from the dead conquering death, sin, and the grave, is that we can come to God and walk to him in our integrity. We can trust in the Lord and because of that faith we shall not slip. We can ask God to examine our hearts and prove us. We can keep God's mercy and loving kindness before our eyes. And if we can learn to pray like that, my friends, if we can, like the publican, say, "God have mercy upon me, a sinner," then we too will walk away justified.

That, however, is not where it ends. You see, if all I came to tell you is that God can forgive you of your sins, that would be great. But there's so much more for you than just justification. And the next part, the part that sounded rudest to me, was about that. Because I found that after I'd given my life to Christ, after he'd washed away my sins and brought me into communion with him, I had a lot of work to do. I had to stop sitting with idolatrous mortals. I had to stop going in with hypocrites. I had to begin to hate the sin that I used to participate in. I had to change my friend circles and the people I spent my time with. Because after justification, my friends, comes sanctification.

You see, when Jesus has transformed your life, when he's made you one with himself, it's not just a one-time event; it's an entire lifetime of being made more like Christ. You begin to hate your sin as you grow in love of God and in love of neighbor. Paul says it like this in Romans 6. He says: "But now having been set free from sin, and having become slaves of God, you have your fruit unto sanctification and in the end eternal life" (v. 22).

You wash your hands in innocence. You go about the altar. And knowing all that God has done for you, you're finally set free to open your mouth and begin telling everybody about the wondrous works of God. You might think that that's not what people want to hear today. People don't want to hear about sin and repentance and salvation. But I can only tell you what I know. I know that Christ came to save sinners. And if you're not a sinner, my friend, I can't help you. But if you are, I've got great news for you. Not only will Jesus cleanse you of your sin, but he will take away all unrighteousness (1 John 1:9). He will cast your sins as far as the east is from the west, as far as the heavens are above the earth (Ps 103:12; Isa 55:9). And he will help you every single day to become more and more like Christ until you reach perfection.

That's a tough word, isn't it? How can anyone be perfect? Peter tells us in 2 Peter 1, that we can have the divine nature of Christ (v. 4). Athanasius said it like this, that God became man so that man could become God. But maybe you'll prefer Wesley's words. He said, "go on to perfection." Keep going, keep seeking God, keep reading God's Word, keep praying. Stay in communion with the people that God has put around you to strengthen you in your faith. And in doing so, you'll find that one day you can come before God and say, "do not gather my soul with sinners, nor my life with the bloodthirsty" (Ps 26:9). You'll have a blessed assurance in your heart that Jesus is yours and know that you don't have to worry about the day you close your eyes. You can stand in an even place, all your hope firmly grounded in Christ. And then you can finally say, "Bless me, Lord. After all, I deserve it. Not because I'm good, but because you've justified me by faith, you've sanctified me by grace, and you've perfected me in love."

Thanks be to God. Amen.

CHAPTER IX

Psalm 58

Hip-hop and rude praise

Shadrach Kabango

Psalm 58

To the leader: Do Not Destroy. Of David. A Miktam.

1 Do you indeed decree what is right, you gods?
Do you judge people fairly?
2 No, in your hearts you devise wrongs;
your hands deal out violence on earth.

3 The wicked go astray from the womb;
they err from their birth, speaking lies.
4 They have venom like the venom of a serpent,
like the deaf adder that stops its ear,
5 so that it does not hear the voice of charmers
or of the cunning enchanter.

6 O God, break the teeth in their mouths;
tear out the fangs of the young lions, O LORD!
7 Let them vanish like water that runs away;
like grass let them be trodden down and wither.
8 Let them be like the snail that dissolves into slime,
like the untimely birth that never sees the sun.

[9] Sooner than your pots can feel the heat of thorns,
whether green or ablaze, may he sweep them away!

[10] The righteous will rejoice when they see vengeance done;
they will bathe their feet in the blood of the wicked.
[11] People will say, "Surely there is a reward for the righteous;
surely there is a God who judges on earth."

THIS IS EXACTLY THE second time I've ever preached, so I hope you like live experiments. I told Jason that I'd never preached before and all the usual caveats, and he signed the waiver, and the one thing I asked for was some parameters. As an artist, I like to work within limits. And he gave me this theme of rude praise, which is just really evocative, as well as this beautiful scripture also to reflect on. So, I'm happy to share my thoughts on these two things. I've spent much of my life inhabiting the world of hip-hop music as an artist, as a fan, and also as part of a documentary project called *Hip-Hop Evolution* that chronicles the history of hip-hop.

Now I've also spent all of my life in the church as a practicing Christian. To some, these two worlds couldn't seem more disparate. And there are tensions to be sure, but they've never felt contradictory to me. I've always sensed quite a bit of overlap actually. And one of those places of overlap you could say is around this idea of rude praise. Let's start with rudeness. That's the fun one. I'll talk about praise as well. But let's start with rudeness. A common topic of conversation around rap music is the language—the explicit language, the rude language. Actually, those little "explicit language" stickers, if any of you are from the music-buying generation, as I am (who can remember buying music?), sometimes they had these little stickers on them that had content warnings. That actually started with hip-hop.

There was a rap album in the '80s by a group called Two Live Crew that was initially banned outright from sale. And when the group appealed that decision, it went all the way to the Supreme Court, and the legal compromise that was struck was that the album could be sold, but it had to have these stickers, these content warnings that say, "explicit content," mature content. Keep that in the back of your minds, we'll come back to it later. But yes, hip-hop is indeed the most profane, provocative musical genre going.

Some of that content I choose not to consume, but it's not the language per se that stops me from consuming it. What people must understand is that language in hip-hop is not at all bound by the rules of polite society because it was created by people who were never included in or much helped by polite society. It was created by kids who were largely ignored by folks who have excellent etiquette. It was created by youth who were left to rot and die by people with extraordinary manners. So, there's always been a deliberate, gleeful flaunting of these people's rules in hip-hop, their arbitrary codes of conduct, their sense of what is and isn't rude. And in doing so, hip-hop exposes those rules, exposes those codes as often being a facade, at best, and hypocrisy, at worst.

Precisely the kind of hypocrisy that Jesus called out, is it not? And Jesus called it out sometimes in similarly provocative ways, by the way, sometimes with similarly straight-up rude language. The Pharisees were people who observed all the rules and customs in Jesus' time, proper conduct to a T. And in Matthew 12:34, Jesus calls the Pharisees "a brood of vipers," which means children of Satan, to be perfectly clear. Not a nice phrase. I'm not sure if it would have been considered a curse word, but certainly colorful language from our Lord and Savior.

The scriptures also tell us that Jesus once used a whip to drive traders out of the temple and then proceeded to do some light to medium property damage, flipping the tables of the moneylenders (John 2:13–17). Rude behavior, rudeness, praise.

What is rude? What is praise? Rap music interrogates this. Jesus interrogates this. And I believe we're called to do the same. Mark chapter 3 starts like this:

> Again he entered the synagogue, and a man was there who had a withered hand. They were watching him to see whether he would cure him on the Sabbath, so that they might accuse him. And he said to the man who had the withered hand, "Come forward." Then he said to them, "Is it lawful to do good or to do harm on the Sabbath, to save life or to kill?" But they were silent. He looked around

> at them with anger; he was grieved at their hardness of heart and said to the man, "Stretch out your hand." He stretched it out, and his hand was restored. The Pharisees went out and immediately conspired with the Herodians against him, how to destroy him. (Mark 3:1–6)

And we know what Jesus did after that.

In 1988, a rap group from LA recorded a song that I will call in this space, "F— the Police." And polite society was up in arms. But what the group was saying, what they were interrogating was: What is lawful? What is more rude? What is more morally objectionable? Decrying injustice with some colorful language or racist police brutality? A bad word conveying righteous anger or the countless instances of our people being mistreated or even killed by the very people tasked to serve and protect us?

Those lyrics and that song title that I just quoted remind me also of Psalm 58, which we just heard, and also of Psalm 137, which says:

> By the rivers of Babylon—we sat and wept when we remembered Zion. There on the poplars we hung our harps, for there our captors asked us for songs, our tormentors demanded songs of joy. They said, sing us one of the songs of Zion. How can we sing the songs of the LORD while in a foreign land? If I forget you, Jerusalem, may my right hand forget its skill. May my tongue cling to the roof of my mouth if I do not remember you, if I do not consider Jerusalem my highest joy. Remember, LORD, what the Edomites did on the day Jerusalem fell. Tear it down, they cried. Tear it down to its foundations. Daughter Babylon, doomed to destruction, happy is the one who repays you according to what you have done. Happy is the one who seizes your infants and dashes them against the rock!

If I wasn't literally quoting scriptures with that last line, I would not feel okay saying that in a church. But it's canon, and it's part of our sacred text for a reason. For those who know injustice, this kind of expression is real. It's cathartic. However rude it may be, it is honest expression of anguish. And for those who have been fortunate enough to never be under the kind of oppression that stirs up a song like this, this passage says, listen. It says, don't ignore. It says, withhold your judgment. Do not police the language.

Listen.

The church doesn't always do a fabulous job of this kind of listening. We ignore psalms like Psalm 137 or Psalm 58. We skip over Jesus cursing the fig tree, destroying business people's property, hurling painful insults. Now there's a lot of psalms in the Bible. I can understand skipping a few here and there. But we often miss the main story of our faith because of our aversion to rudeness.

The only other time I was ever asked to preach, I gave a talk the night before in the same church. And I spoke about an album that I'd made, an album called *A Short Story About a War* (2018). It's a concept album. It had all these different characters in it. It had a revolutionary army, a state army, snipers, and so on. And after I was done giving this talk, sort of unpacking this album, there was a Q&A period. And someone stood up and asked, how do you feel as a Christian telling this violent story?

And I looked behind me and pointed out: That's a giant crucifix.

A rap album might have received the first explicit content sticker, but the story of Jesus should have gotten it a long time ago. It's extraordinarily raw. It's gory. It's not just violent. You could argue that it's about violence, about our violence, the world's violence, our sin, and God coming into the muck and the mess and the rudeness of all of it with his rescuing love. It's absolutely about politics; it's about religion and power; it's about hypocrisy; it's about all the muck of life.

So again, I've never felt that much tension—as much tension as people think—inhabiting the worlds of hip-hop and the church because people generally think of hip-hop as being ruder than it really is and think of scripture as a lot more polite than it really is. Why is that?

Racism would probably be reasons one through six or seven, and it's important to recognize that and deal with it. But maybe more importantly, we should ask, what does this misreading, this misunderstanding, do to us?

A couple of things. One, I think it makes us feel more safe when everything is good, but it doesn't make us feel more comforted when everything is not. Because we tell ourselves that our religious tradition and our savior were never rude, never expressed anger, never expressed a desire for justice, never called out hypocrisy in clear and even creative terms.

I think we also secondly fail to understand our world because we're not looking at the ancient world for what it was, which is not that different from ours in many important ways. There are political powers, there are rich and poor, and there's devoutly religious people who are badly missing the point. Yesterday, just like today.

On the album I just mentioned, *A Short Story About a War*, I wrote a song called "The Stone Throwers." "The Stone Throwers" are this group I imagine that had no access to any real weapons so they could only throw stones. And their violence was therefore brutal and visceral, not like precise sniper shots or drone strikes. But this isn't because they're more savage or inhumane people. In fact, in the grand scheme, they actually do much less violence than the more respectable, powerful armies with their sophisticated, advanced weapons.

The first verse of that song goes like this:

> Game hasn't changed, same ol' monopoly
> Same couple players own all of the property
> I ain't a prop, don't give no props to me
> My people still don't eat properly
> Think we forgot? We was just property
> Think we'll be bought again?
> Think that they brought them democracy?
> I think they brought back them poppy seeds
> My people locked up for chopping
> That's hypocrisy
> We wasn't thought of
> We wasn't brought up and taught we was set up
> That's why we get caught up
> Y'all discarded us

Put them bars up
Of course we got guards up
We hard cuz we're hard up
They got them start-ups and Starbucks
We got a couple of stars till they turn 'em to stardust
They starve us
Can't even drink water
Up North with that Flint water
All in the sink as they sink farther
Kids on the brink
Y'all went to Harvard and Stanford
Think harder for answers man, think
We're far below standards
Don't tell me anger won't help us
You told me the cancer would shrink
We need a shrink
We just see boys making bands: N'Sync
Open your eyes my fam, we all could be gone in a blink

The video for that song consisted of black bodies standing in different iconic places in Toronto, completely naked. Not as show of rudeness, but actually as show of vulnerability. The scriptures describe Jesus as naked on the cross, but he's rarely depicted that way. Why? What do we lose when we tidy up the graphic nature that's at the center of our faith?

I've talked for a while about rudeness in rap and in scripture, and I want to talk now a little bit about praise.

First of all, in hip-hop and in all art, praise is woven throughout. Affirmation, admiration, these feelings are, in my view, inherent in art. Even expressing the harshest realities in the harshest terms is fundamentally life-affirming, in my view, because it's an attempt to reach out. Even the grittiest, grimiest hip-hop is taking the darkness of life and bringing it into the light. And that is the crucial first step. Maybe the same way we don't get to resurrection without first encountering death, we don't get real praise without first encountering rudeness. But a lot of times we want to get to the praise without having to get into the rude stuff. We want the melody to resolve at the end of every single chorus. We want a happy ending to every single story, but that's just not real. I'm no

Bible scholar, but I don't think that's biblical either. Psalm 137 that I just read does not lyrically resolve to praise, as we just heard. It ends with just about as rude a thing as you can possibly say.

The story of David, who wrote many of the psalms, does not resolve perfectly. In the end, he doesn't get to build a temple to Yahweh because of the bloodshed during his reign (1 Chr 22:8). And his successor is a child that he had with the mistress whose husband he famously killed. It's not the neatest resolution I've ever heard. Noah's story certainly has no joyous resolution. It's super strange at the end. Jacob's story was just kind of rude and strange throughout. Of course, a whole lot of disciples were killed. John the Baptist was beheaded. Paul and Silas were tossed in prison. Jesus, naked, with nails in his hands and feet, asked why his Father had forsaken him.

Long story short: There's a lot of rudeness before the praise. There's a lot of praise within the rudeness.

So why does our sense of what constitutes praise sometimes feel so small? It doesn't ring true for me; it doesn't ring true for most people. What does is often a simple reading of the Psalms or, of course, hip-hop. I've been talking a bit about hip-hop's strong political voice speaking out about injustice, but hip-hop actually started as party music. I'm biased, but nothing can enliven and excite quite like hip-hop music. The earliest lyrics in rap were all about praising the DJ, praising the party, praising the partygoers, playfully, defiantly celebrating self, in a world that often dismisses and diminishes us, even though we too are God's fearfully and wonderfully made creatures (Ps 139:14).

So, the same way I asked, what do we lose when we judge or ignore the rudeness in scripture or in culture?, I now ask: What happens when we have a small sense of what praise has to sound like? What does it mean when we need the explicit content of life to quickly resolve to something G-rated and cheerful?

Well, firstly, I think it means that we're not trusting God to reconcile all things in his own way and in his own time. I think it means we think God is only in the beautiful praise and not also, or even more, in the ugly tears. And certainly not both at once. One thing I love about hip-hop is that it's both at once. And Jesus, we believe, was also both at once, God and man. The Son of Man came eating and drinking and was called a drunkard and a friend of tax collectors and sinners, as it says in Matthew 11:19. And yet we believe that he was also somehow God.

Kendrick Lamar—a rapper who's won everything from a Grammy to a Pulitzer to a recent battle with Drake—had a hit song in 2015 where he rapped, and I will paraphrase here for church reasons: I'm effed up, homie; you're effed up; but if God's got us, then we gon' be all right. We gon' be all right. That's rude praise.

We don't sing that in churches, but they sang it in the streets in 2016 and onwards in the movement for justice for Black lives. It was the anthem. It was a kind of praise, rude praise that resonated with people, that rang true.

We've asked what is rude today, but let's quickly also ask what is praise? What is worship? In Isaiah 58:3–4, it says:

> Why have we fasted, they say, and you have not seen it? Why have we humbled ourselves and you have not noticed? Yet on the day of our fasting, you do as you please and exploit all your workers. Your fasting ends in quarreling and strife and in striking each other with wicked fists. You cannot fast as you do today and expect your voice to be heard on high.

Isaiah 1:11–17 says:

> The multitude of your sacrifices, what are they to me, says the Lord. I have more than enough of burnt offerings of rams and the fat of fattened animals. I have no pleasure in the blood of bulls and lambs and goats. When you come to appear before me, who has asked this of you, this trampling of my courts? Stop bringing meaningless offerings. Your incense is detestable to me. New moons, Sabbaths, and convocations, I cannot bear your worthless assemblies. Your new moon feasts and your appointed festivals, I hate with all my being. They have become a burden to me. I am wary of bearing them. When you spread out your hands in prayer, I hide my eyes from you. Even when you offer many prayers, I am not listening. Your hands are full of blood.

> Wash and make yourselves clean. Take your evil deeds out of my sight. Stop doing wrong. Learn to do right. Seek justice, defend the oppressed, take up the cause of the fatherless, plead the case of the widow.

What is worship?

What is praise? James says, "Religion that God our Father accepts as pure and faultless is this, to look after orphans and widows in their distress and to keep oneself from being polluted by the world" (1:27).

Where I landed on all this reflecting on rudeness and praise is an important musical concept called *listening*.

One of the greatest rappers of all time goes by name of Andre 3000. He made virtuosic futuristic music in the '90s with his brilliant partner Big Boy and a group called Outkast. And on his first solo single called "Hey Ya," he made a pop song that somehow synthesized decades of music into three perfect minutes. Completely outside of hip-hop. The song went to number one on Billboard, and he was hailed as a genius. And around that time, I remember an interviewer asked him what he thought about all the adulation and this genius title that was being applied to him. And I remember he looked at her very seriously and soberly, no false humility in his eyes. He said, "I'm not a genius. I know I'm not a genius because I know how hard I work."

He said, "I just pay attention."

I'd like to end on that note because as any artist will tell you, the most important skill in music, hip-hop or otherwise, is not the ability to make beautiful noise, it's the ability to listen, to pay attention. Obviously a very important skill in social life, we all know, but it's an equally important skill in our interior spiritual life. Can we listen? Especially to pain, especially to the rudeness of scriptures, of our own hearts and lives, and of those around us? And can we hear praise, even in the melodies and stories that have no simple resolution? And can we hear them together, the rude praise? Can we live with the paradoxes and complexities that produce the richest music, the greatest compassion, the deepest faith? May we all have ears to hear.

CHAPTER X

Genesis 18:22–33

Prayer as negotiation: Holy *chutzpah!*

Rabbi Yael Splansky

"Sleeps and Slumbers, The Guardian of Israel"

by Rabbi Rivkah Lubitch

רבקה לוביץ
שיר לנפילות
נשאתי עיני אל ההרים ולא בא עזרי

I LIFTED MY EYES to the mountains, but my help did not come. I had no help from God, maker of heaven and earth.

> 22 So the men turned from there and went toward Sodom, while Abraham remained standing before the LORD.
> 23 Then Abraham came near and said, "Will you indeed sweep away the righteous with the wicked? 24 Suppose there are fifty righteous within the city; will you then sweep away the place and not forgive it for the fifty righteous who are in it? 25 Far be it from you to do such a thing, to slay the righteous with the wicked, so that the righteous fare as the wicked! Far be that from you! Shall not the Judge of all the earth do what is just?" 26 And the

> Lord said, "If I find at Sodom fifty righteous in the city, I will forgive the whole place for their sake." 27 Abraham answered, "Let me take it upon myself to speak to my lord, I who am but dust and ashes. 28 Suppose five of the fifty righteous are lacking? Will you destroy the whole city for lack of five?" And he said, "I will not destroy it if I find forty-five there." 29 Again he spoke to him, "Suppose forty are found there." He answered, "For the sake of forty I will not do it." 30 Then he said, "Oh, do not let my lord be angry if I speak. Suppose thirty are found there." He answered, "I will not do it, if I find thirty there." 31 He said, "Let me take it upon myself to speak to my lord. Suppose twenty are found there." He answered, "For the sake of twenty I will not destroy it." 32 Then he said, "Oh, do not let my lord be angry if I speak just once more. Suppose ten are found there." He answered, "For the sake of ten I will not destroy it." 33 And the Lord went his way, when he had finished speaking to Abraham, and Abraham returned to his place.

Chutzpah is a Talmudic Hebrew word that has made its way into Yiddish and then from there into American slang. My great grandfather, who loved the colorful language of Yiddish, would laugh out loud to know that the word *chutzpah* has now been included in the Oxford English Dictionary. To my surprise, though, only the negative connotation of the word is provided there. *Chutzpah* has two meanings and can be used in two ways, one negative and one positive.

Oxford defines *chutzpah* as impudence or even arrogance. In Israel, you might hear one customer in line scold another pushy customer in line with the words, *"Eizeh Chutz-PAH!"*: Some nerve. That's a good use of the word in its negative sense. But what Oxford misses is that *chutzpah* is also a way of describing an admirable trait. When someone shows gumption, we might say, that took real guts. That was a gutsy decision. That took *chutzpah*.

Now, humility and modesty and patience are, of course, also Jewish values. And there is a time and a place when *chutzpah* is necessary and the most effective way to respond. It is this positive attribute that shows up again and again in Jewish prayer. And that's what I would like to speak with you a little bit about today. I call it holy *chutzpah.*

The two sides of *chutzpah* are echoed in the two sides of the biblical expression used to describe the Jewish people. You may recall how God refers to the Israelites as *"Am K'shey Oref,"* a stiff-necked people. The rabbinic commentators throughout the centuries debate whether this is an insult or perhaps a compliment.

Could being stiff-necked, could knowing when to stick your neck out, be the very secret of our survival? Precisely because we are unwilling to give up on God, because we refuse to give up on life, because we won't give up on humanity, because we will not forfeit hope in the future, because we continue to pray even when God is silent, even when God seems absent. This is the *chutzpah* that has seen the Jewish people through four thousand years.

We could say it all began with Abraham, Genesis 18, as we heard. So faithful and so full of *chutzpah* was our father Abraham that he stepped forward in the presence of God, *Vayegash Avraham,* and then addressed God directly. הַאַף תִּסְפֶּה צַדִּיק עִם־רָשָׁע׃ "Will you sweep away the innocent along with the guilty?"

Abraham finds his voice fueled with righteous outrage and makes his demands with accusation and scolding. You can hear it even better in the Hebrew. *Chalilah Lecha!* Far be it from you to do such a thing, to bring death upon the innocent as well as the guilty so that innocent and guilty fare alike. *Chalilah Lecha!* It literally means it would be a desecration for you. And not only does God take it, but God seems to be proud of Abraham's righteous indignation, his holy *chutzpah.*

Now it doesn't change the facts on the ground. Destruction will rain down on the evil cities of Sodom and Gomorrah, but Abraham shows us what the fair fight of the faithful sounds like. Another example from the scriptures that we share.

When we were leaving Egypt, Pharaoh's army approaching from our backs, the sea raging in front of us: What happened then? Torah tells us that Moses raised his staff. But according to rabbinic imagination, there's another character in the scene. He's named for us in scripture, Nahshon, the son of Aminadav. But we know nothing about him. No ink is wasted in Torah, so this man must have had a significant role to play. Our sages teach, through the power of imagination, that at just that moment, when Moses raises his staff, nothing, no miracle.

So, Nahshon ben Aminadav walks into the water and says, *Mi Chamocha BaEilim, Adonai*, who is like you, Adonai, among the gods who are worshiped? And he continues to walk with the waters rising to his knees, to his hips. And just when the water is at his neck, he calls out that second verse of the song, *Mi Kamocha*—that's why the "*Chamocha*" changes to "*Kamocha,*" because the water is filling his throat—*nedar bakodesh!* "Who is like you, majestic in holiness, awesome in splendor, working wonders?" And only when the water covers his nose, and some say his eyes, do the seas split open for the Israelites to pass to freedom.

Nahshon's prayer is full of *chutzpah*, and it forced a miracle. He made a demand of the Almighty, saying, "You are the only one who can work wonders. So do your job. This is your moment."

Now, sometimes it works and sometimes it doesn't. And God only knows when and why and for whom. But that must not keep us from trying. Our prayer book is filled with holy *chutzpah*.

One example: *Asher Yatzar*, a morning prayer that we offer privately, asking for our bodies to function well. It literally is a prayer for plumbing. We say, "*n'kavim n'kavim, chalulim chalulim*": may the parts that should be open remain open, may the parts that should be closed remain closed. Some of you may know what I'm talking about. *Baruch Ata*, praised are you, O God, who made the human form with wisdom. You have created an intricate system of valves and vital organs—And now here comes the *chutzpah*—It is well known before you on high. If even one of these systems were to fail, it would be impossible for me to rise up and stand before you and praise your holy Name. *Baruch Atah*, praised are you, healer of all flesh and maker of wonders.

Did you catch the implied threat? If you do not sustain this body of mine, I won't be able to get out of bed and stand strong before you and praise your Name.

Now of course sometimes it works, and sometimes it doesn't. But it doesn't hurt to try. We may get extra points for a passionate *chutzpah*-infused plea. How do we fulfill the commandment to love God with all the heart? Every day we chant from Deuteronomy. A rabbinic anthology of commentaries from the third century in Israel suggests that "with all your heart" means "with an *undivided* heart." When you turn Godward and cry out, let it be wholeheartedly.

I inherited a book from my predecessor, Rabbi Dov Marmur of blessed memory, and I treasure every note that he's written in the margin, every phrase that he underlined, every page corner he turned down for emphasis—as if leaving instruction for me. You see, Rabbi Marmur was a child survivor of the Holocaust, and the title of his book is *Facing the Abusing God: A Theology of Protest*. The author, Rabbi David Blumenthal, asks: How do you love the eternal, your God, with all your heart? And he answer: By allowing yourself to be silenced by the presence of God, a silence of amazement and receptivity. And by not allowing yourself to remain silenced by God, by taking up speech, which is strong and just.[1]

We see a shining example of this in the Hasidic master Rabbi Levi Yitzchak of Berdichev. He lived in Poland and Ukraine in the eighteenth century, when life was often dark and bloody for my people. And nevertheless, the Berdichev Rabbi had an open line to God, and he knew how to use it. He said, "Good morning to you, Master of the universe. I, Levi Yitzchak, the son of Sarah of Berdichev, I come to you with a formal complaint, a legal matter from your people Israel. What do you want from your people Israel? What have you demanded of your people Israel? Everywhere it is written, speak to the children of Israel, demand of the children of Israel, command of the children of Israel. And so, I ask you, compassionate Father in heaven, how many nations are there in the world? Babylonians, Persians, Edomites, the Russians, what do they say? They say that their tsar is the only ruler, supreme. And the Prussians, what do they say? That their kaiser is the ruler,

1. David Blumenthal, *Facing the Abusing God: A Theology of Protest* (Louisville: Westminster/John Knox, 1993).

supreme. And the English, what do they say? That George III is sovereign. And so, I, Levi Yitzchak, son of Sarah of Berdichev, what do I say? *Yisgadal veyiskadash shemei rabah*, magnified and sanctified is your holy Name. And therefore, I, Levi Yitzchak, son of Sarah of Berdychiv, I say from this place I will not move. I will not waver from this spot until there be an end to all this suffering, until there be an end to this exile. *Yisgadal veyiskadash shemei rabbah*, magnified and sanctified in only your Name."

Now, how long did the Rabbi of Berdichev stand there? I do not know. But the story, the story still stands. His shining example of holy *chutzpah* endures so that we might emulate it. One important day on the Jewish calendar is Tish'a Ba'av, the ninth day of the month of Av when we mourn the destruction of the first temple that stood in Jerusalem in 586 BCE, when the Babylonians breached the walls of the Holy City. They set the temple to torch and our people were taken into exile by the rivers of Babylon. There we wept as we remembered Zion. And on this single day, we also mourn the destruction of Jerusalem's second temple.

In the year 70 of the Common Era, the Romans carried my people in chains for an exile that would last two thousand years. This year, many Jews will observe Tish B'av as they never did before. Many will fast. Many will sit on the floor to chant from the biblical Book of Lamentations. They may pray a full-hearted prayer for the protection of Israel and all her inhabitants. Because you see, on October 7th, the protective wall was breached. Homes were set to torch. Whole families were burned alive. Hundreds of people, including children and elders, were taken captive. One hundred thousand were displaced by rockets subsequently.

So new *chutzpah*-inflected prayers are being written now. New poems of lament, new songs intended to force a miracle. I'll share just one with you. Rabbi Rivka Lubitsch from Israel Center for Women's Justice takes up this long thread of honest and accusing voice, which runs throughout Jewish history, in the shadow of October 7th brutal assaults against women. Rabbi Rivkah takes Psalm 121 and inverts it. She turns it on its head. You know how it begins: "I lift up mine eyes to the hills." It continues as in the epigraph above.

> I lifted my eyes to the mountains,
>   but my help did not come.
> I had no help from God,
>   maker of heaven and earth."

This is one model of prayer that continues to weave its way through the fabric of Jewish history. And we are strengthened by it. We are reinforced by it. Our courage to face the future, our courage to hold on to hope, needs such a demanding prayer.

It is brutally honest prayer. It is prayer that presumes that God needs human beings like us, like you and me, to point and to say, this is the one God of the universe, the only one. So, if God desires our prayer, then it is fair game to leverage that desire. This prayer tradition asserts that when we suffer, we must not suffer alone. We must not shut God out from our cries. This prayer tradition has never been afraid to go there because God Almighty can take it; for all we know, God may even be longing for it.

If we take our suffering seriously, if we take our relationship with God seriously, if we take human history and our role in it seriously, let us find our way to bring an extra measure of gumption to our prayers. Let us show faith in the hard truths, faith in the hard questions, faith in those who raise the hard questions. And faith in God who listens for our questioning.

Once upon a time, the sea split and we, the people of Israel, marveled at your outstretched arm. We will live on memories of newfound joy, stubborn and stiff-necked. We will cling to hope and gather strength to fight the Pharaohs when we must and hold fast to freedom for all and celebrate in song and vow that we will never be among the silenced or the silent.

CHAPTER XI

Luke 6:27–36

Jesus: Ridiculous and rude

Rev. Jaylynn Byassee

Luke 6:27–36

27 I say to you who are listening: Love your enemies; do good to those who hate you; 28 bless those who curse you; pray for those who mistreat you. 29 If anyone strikes you on the cheek, offer the other also, and from anyone who takes away your coat do not withhold even your shirt. 30 Give to everyone who asks of you, and if anyone takes away what is yours, do not ask for it back again. 31 Do to others as you would have them do to you.

32 "If you love those who love you, what credit is that to you? For even sinners love those who love them. 33 If you do good to those who do good to you, what credit is that to you? For even sinners do the same. 34 If you lend to those from whom you expect to receive payment, what credit is that to you? Even sinners lend to sinners, to receive as much again. 35 Instead, love your enemies, do good, and lend, expecting nothing in return. Your reward will be great, and you will be children of the Most High, for he himself is kind to the ungrateful and the wicked. 36 Be merciful, just as your Father is merciful.

As I thought about the most rude passages I know, this one from Luke's Gospel came to mind. Jesus gets right to the point in Luke and starts these verses in chapter 6 with the summary of the whole—love your enemies—and then proceeds to unpack it for us.

So, yeah, love your enemies is about the hardest thing we can do. Then being good to those who hate us, blessing and praying for the most difficult people in our lives and loving them. And believe me, whether we admit it or not, there are some people we don't really want to love—it's really difficult! And each sentence that you heard read from today's scripture just seemed to get harder and harder to accept. It doesn't get any easier to hear them. It simply would've been easiest if Jesus had just left this bit of instruction off the table. Feels rude of him to ask us to do something so ridiculous. Something that makes no sense.

So here we are.

You have already considered the words of the wonderful Shadrach Kabango (Shad K), who preached the good Word, encouraging us to listen (see chapter IX). We're better at listening when it's what we want to hear. If I'm honest, I'm *not* ready to hear this scripture today. Which is why I know we probably should. I'd prefer the passage to open with the words "Avoid your enemies." I think we could do that pretty good! To love them is a little rude of Jesus to expect. Actually, just plain ridiculous. Who does that? And why should we?

Well, I'm going to age myself here, but I'm okay with embracing age. In the early '90s, there was a Gatorade commercial with a jingle that said, "Be Like Mike." It was at the height of Michael Jordan's career, and the commercial was made primarily to have children emulate him. After the wonderful Paris Olympics of 2024, we might update Nike: "Be like Summer McIntosh, or Simone Biles." But we're not here to emulate athletes. We can admire them! I already miss the Olympics! But we are encouraged throughout Luke's Gospel, to be *like* God.

If we lived such a life, if *everyone* lived such a life, where we loved our enemies and gave without expecting return, and blessed those who curse us, and so on, there would be no violence, no revenge, no jealousy, no adamant distinctions between property and possessions, no divisions between class or caste. But we know that that's not the world we live in. As Christians, we're called to be like God. God's Word remains true, and we may think it's some wild, rude instruction. Maybe it is. But often what seems like a ridiculous request of Jesus, is precisely what defines how we praise our God.

So, how do we love our enemies? In today's culture, if you have a public enemy, everyone knows it—social media has raised the hype of sharing hatred like it's just another part of your day. If there's an enemy on the loose, chances are we see them as evil, and we don't want any part of them. But then there's this Gospel of Luke, and this thing about Jesus teaching us how to live. And part of that living is having a love for enemies and those who aren't so nice to us. Or maybe we're the ones who are not so nice to others. Have we ever considered that we might be an enemy to those we neglect and ignore?

When my family was on a sabbatical in England a few years ago, Jason and I visited various churches that were doing refugee support in their communities. One of these small towns had a church that was overflowing with people—almost all of them refugees. Prior to the refugee-welcoming minister's arrival, the church was about to close its doors for good.

The pastor told us that when he accepted the ministry position, his colleagues warned him not to go. The town was not known for its vitality. In fact, it had a depressing reputation. They told this pastor, "You don't want to move your family there. The schools are horrible, and the city is drab." The pastor thought, "Well, it's not the schools or the city that I'm called to, it's the people." And he realized that if he didn't take the position as the minister of this church in this town, he would essentially be protecting his own children *from Jesus*. To *not go* was avoiding the very reason Jesus needed him to go: to love others.

It's easy to love those who love us already. And it's not hard to do good to those who do good to us. But Jesus asks us to do what is not easy. To love where there may not be love in return, or kindness back. Ever. In this lifetime. But to follow and love like Jesus loves, we will be transformed in new ways. It's inevitable!

This "love your enemy" command doesn't mean kill them with kindness, and they'll *finally* come around, and you'll get your way, and they'll do what you want. This is different. This is prayer for the one with whom we disagree. This could be as simple as a work colleague that you see every day. I was a special needs education teacher back in my younger adult days. I worked with children who had emotional disabilities and came from troubled places and homes. The shelf life for these kinds of teachers is about three years before they hit burnout. I remember working with a counselor for a specific child. I was the instructor, but she was doing the therapy. I disagreed with her approach. And every day I came to work, I felt more and more bitter. Until finally, I just decided to pray for the counselor—every day. And then, surprisingly, I liked her better. My insides weren't twisted with bitterness, but I felt more compassion for her and for her role in these kids' lives. I don't remember how we finally approached the child, but I do know the child was better cared for as a result of our relationship being healed. Someone once said, "I prayed and prayed for my enemies, until one day I realized they were no longer my enemies anymore."

Stanley Hauerwas, one of the greatest theologians of our time, has another take. He writes that just because we're told to forgive and love our enemies, does not mean that they will cease being our enemies! That tracks, too. We can't control others' responses, but we have some control over ours. "Be like God," Jesus urges.

If someone is difficult, pray for that person. That doesn't necessarily mean that we allow the pain, or abuse, or any sort of actions that harm us. But pray. When we do, we realize that we can't possibly accept them in our own strength, but only with strength from God. Through prayer, which brings the Holy Spirit, we might have new life and love for the journey. Now that's a different kind of strength. That's something to give praise for.

Where in our world, and in our history, have we seen enemy-love work? Back when there was apartheid in South Africa, there were churches that stood for love of Black and White South

Africans, and for reconciliation. Nelson Mandela wanted a country based on forgiveness, not a bloodbath. The Rev. Dr. Peter Storey (my professor in seminary) was a Methodist minister during that time, and he is a White South African. He was chaplain to Nelson Mandela on Robben Island. Robben Island is now a place where tourists can go. Peter can't. The memory of that place is too painful. Storey's entire ministry in South Africa was shaped by one simple question: What does it mean to obey Jesus in apartheid South Africa? And he tried in profound ways to live into the answer each day. What does it mean for us, friends, to obey Jesus, *where we live*, by loving our enemies? What might come of it if we do? Nelson Mandela, in his autobiography, writes, "No one is born hating another person because of the color of skin, religion, [or culture], . . . people are taught to hate. Love comes more naturally."[1] Teach love!

Luke's Gospel gives us words that many in our world have heard—not just Christians: the Golden Rule. Do unto others as you would have them do unto you. But we don't always do that well. How do we treat others?

In ancient times, relationships were often built on an exchange of gifts. I suppose you could say the same for today. Friendships were forged through evenly reciprocating each other's gifts. I was talking with a friend of mine. He's Chinese, and he mentioned that reciprocation of gifts is very much a part of their lives. He calls it the culture of reciprocity. He said, for example, "If my son graduated and my friend gave him $100, then when my friend's daughter graduated, it is an unspoken understanding that I, in turn, would give her exactly $100." He also laughed about how he and his friends would fight over the bill at a restaurant. And even if you paid last time, you were supposed to fight about paying again. With me, I can never remember who paid last time! So, my friends are mostly out of luck!

In our social worlds, there are often unspoken customs that we practice. And when someone doesn't respond in the way that

1. Nelson Mandela, *Long Walk to Freedom: The Autobiography of Nelson Mandela* (Boston: Back Bay, 1995), 622.

we think they should, we notice. Jesus isn't asking us to do something so that we'll get its equivalent back.

There's a right way to do it—there's just one way: to love. Because that's what God does for us. Love for enemies is one of the strangest things about us Christians. It sets Christians apart. Other religions, including those closest to us, simply disagree. Jesus loves his enemies and dies for the ones who crucified him. That's the heart of our unusual and different story. Flannery O'Connor said: "You shall know the truth, and the truth shall make you odd." Christians follow a risen Lord. That's just going to look different.

Back in biblical times, it also meant a breach of social conventions if someone didn't reciprocate a gift in kind. So it was revolutionary in Luke to treat all persons, no matter their status, the same, as if they all stood as equals, on level ground, like the plains that Jesus stood on to speak. Earlier in chapter 6, Luke says that Jesus had just chosen his twelve disciples, and the first thing he did after that was to come down the mountain and stand "on a level place." That level ground is significant.

Jesus's teachings are revolutionary. They aren't the natural social norm. We don't instinctively "turn the other cheek" if the first one got hit! There was a little boy who was having some trouble in elementary with some bullies. This kept happening, day after day. The parents were at a loss as to what to do, or how to help. Finally, the dad said, "Hey, today, if it happens again, just look him right here between the eyes and give a little punch." (To be honest, the dad was truly kidding.) I'll let you figure out how I know these "parents" so well. When the child came home that day, he was asked about the bully and how the day went. He simply replied, "I took care of it." I mean, right? I'm kinda cheering for that kid. But inside, we parents were mortified. *Did he* really punch the bully? The truth is, he didn't. But somehow, he did "take care of it." Maybe he did turn the other cheek. Maybe he just didn't stick around and found other friends to play with elsewhere on the playground. Whatever he did, the bullying stopped.

What we do with our actions and how we live as Christians should flow out of God's abundance to us. So that if we actually turn the other cheek (instead of a little punch), it can be an act of resistance to evil, and when we keep doing that, the resistance has the power to transform others, and the world. Now that sounds like something to imitate, someone to give praise to.

The inbreaking of God makes a difference in how we respond to other people.

How we approach people flows out of what we practice. And sometimes we simply practice what we and our neighbors have always done. Relating to people in ways that have become familiar to us. Yet, familiarity can often breed contempt. We become so familiar with how we relate to our neighbors, or the cost of living, or unaffordable housing, or the lack of education for all persons, rent, housing, and so on, that we accept it without much thought. We shrug and say, this is just how it is.

God loves us all not because of what we have done, achieved, or claimed, but solely because of who God is. And because of that love, grace transforms us. While the gospel may be good news for all, the gospel isn't always easy. But the gospel is always good. And that good is what Jesus is all about.

Another example of history and enemies is the genocide in Rwanda in 1994. There were two different ethnic groups: Hutu and Tutsi. The Tutsi formed the wealthier, more powerful part of society, while the Hutus formed the lower, poorer part. After the genocide, more than ninety-five thousand children were orphaned. Through an empowerment organization called Zoe Empowers (*zoe* is Greek for life), I was able to be with some of these orphan groups and hear their stories. I was stunned to hear how members of one family had killed members of another family, with the orphans coming from the two different ethnic groups. But, through the profound love and mercy of Jesus, these youth now shared life together and had a transformed love for one another. The Golden Rule: Do unto others as you would have them do to you . . . . But we don't always do that well.

"Rude" and "praise" have been our two words for this summer series. And "rude" simply means offensive, impolite, or ill-mannered. Perhaps you didn't know Jesus was so rude, but there are many who are threatened by such challenges as loving enemies and mixing with those whom society shuns. Jesus is offensive in that way, and some might say ill-mannered. He doesn't stay high on the mountain; he comes down and continues to demonstrate a lowering of self and a love of others to share this golden rule. Not so that we would simply do good to another, or help a neighbor when they fall, but so that we would be transformed, just like those Rwandan orphans were transformed and became friends by the grace of God's love.

Our faith story is first and foremost about God, not about sin. We are not evil people; we are fallen people. All in need of love. C. S. Lewis jokes that there will be three surprises when we get in heaven:

1. Who's there,
2. Who's not there,
3. That *you*'re there!

We're all fallen, and we're all loved. Teach love, not hate.

We weren't meant to live the way that we're witnessing around the world. In our shared humanity, we have more in common than not. But we are divided by our differences. We see this around the world in Gaza, Ukraine, Venezuela, Lebanon, Iran. Differences are exacerbated in our politics here in North America.

This is not a simple love, this loving of one's enemies. We think it's hard to do, but it costs us more not to do it! It hurts everyone. It's like drinking poison and hoping someone else dies. Instead, let us give praise to the one who teaches us to love. The psalmist declares this love in Psalm 136. There are twenty-six verses, and in all twenty-six we find the repeated phrase: God's "steadfast love endures forever."

Through all the rude, through all the praise, God gets the last word. And that word is forever God's love.

I'll close with some inspiration from Pádraig Ó Tuama, an Irish poet and theologian. He about saved my life during COVID when I first discovered him. In his podcast "Poetry Unbound" he reads poetry—not just his own; he reads from all kinds of poets—and then the entire podcast is unpacking the poem: dissecting it, discovering from it, learning from it. Then at the end, he reads the entire poem again, and one can hear it a whole different way, with a little more clarity and understanding. I think this is a beautiful way to study scripture, as well. So, I'll end with a re-read of just the last few verses in Luke's Gospel from *The Message* translation as a summary:

> I tell you, love your enemies. Help and give without expecting a return. You'll never—I promise—regret it. Live out this God-created identity the way our Father lives toward us, generously and graciously, even when we're at our worst. Our God is kind. (6:35–36)

Friends, practice this love, as we would like others to practice it. Our motivation to do so is by the giver of this love for us. Why do we have to love our enemies? Because God does. That is the transforming beauty of our faith. Amen.

CHAPTER XII

Psalms 9–10

Good news for the afflicted

Dr. Joseph Mangina

Psalm 9

To the leader: according to Muth-labben. A Psalm of David.

1 I will give thanks to the LORD with my whole heart;
I will tell of all your wonderful deeds.
2 I will be glad and exult in you;
I will sing praise to your name, O Most High.

3 When my enemies turned back,
they stumbled and perished before you.
4 For you have maintained my just cause;
you have sat on the throne giving righteous judgment.

5 You have rebuked the nations; you have destroyed the wicked;
you have blotted out their name forever and ever.
6 The enemies have vanished in everlasting ruins;
their cities you have rooted out;
the very memory of them has perished.

7 But the LORD sits enthroned forever;
he has established his throne for judgment.
8 He judges the world with righteousness;
he judges the peoples with equity.

9 The LORD is a stronghold for the oppressed,
a stronghold in times of trouble.
10 And those who know your name put their trust in you,
for you, O LORD, have not forsaken those who seek you.

11 Sing praises to the LORD, who dwells in Zion.
Declare his deeds among the peoples.
12 For he who avenges blood is mindful of them;
he does not forget the cry of the afflicted.

13 Be gracious to me, O LORD.
See what I suffer from those who hate me;
you are the one who lifts me up from the gates of death,
14 so that I may recount all your praises
and, in the gates of daughter Zion,
rejoice in your deliverance.
15 The nations have sunk in the pit that they made;
in the net that they hid has their own foot been caught.
16 The LORD has made himself known; he has executed judgment;
the wicked are snared in the work of their own hands.
Higgaion. *Selah*

17 The wicked shall depart to Sheol,
all the nations that forget God.

18 For the needy shall not always be forgotten,
nor the hope of the poor perish forever.

19 Rise up, O LORD! Do not let mortals prevail;
let the nations be judged before you.
20 Put them in fear, O LORD;
let the nations know that they are only human. *Selah*

Psalm 10

1 Why, O LORD, do you stand far off?
Why do you hide yourself in times of trouble?
2 In arrogance the wicked persecute the poor—
let them be caught in the schemes they have devised.

[3] For the wicked boast of the desires of their heart;
those greedy for gain curse and renounce the Lord.
[4] In the pride of their countenance the wicked say,
"God will not seek it out";
all their thoughts are, "There is no God."

[5] Their ways prosper at all times;
your judgments are on high, out of their sight;
as for their foes, they scoff at them.
[6] They think in their heart, "We shall not be moved;
throughout all generations we shall not meet adversity."

[7] Their mouths are filled with cursing and deceit and oppression;
under their tongues are mischief and iniquity.
[8] They sit in ambush in the villages;
in hiding places they murder the innocent.

Their eyes stealthily watch for the helpless;
[9] they lurk in secret like a lion in its den;
they lurk that they may seize the poor;
they seize the poor and drag them off in their net.

[10] They stoop, they crouch,
and the helpless fall by their might.
[11] They think in their heart, "God has forgotten;
he has hidden his face; he will never see it."

[12] Rise up, O Lord; O God, lift up your hand;
do not forget the oppressed.
[13] Why do the wicked renounce God
and say in their hearts, "You will not call us to account"?

[14] But you do see! Indeed, you note trouble and grief,
that you may take it into your hands;
the helpless commit themselves to you;
you have been the helper of the orphan.

[15] Break the arm of the wicked and evildoers;
seek out their wickedness until you find none.
[16] The Lord is king forever and ever;
the nations shall perish from his land.

[17] O LORD, you will hear the desire of the meek;
you will strengthen their heart; you will incline your ear
[18] to do justice for the orphan and the oppressed,
so that those from earth may strike terror no more.

SOME OF YOU MAY know the writings of Anne Lamott, who is a highly regarded American novelist and essayist. A time came in her life when she was going through an especially difficult patch, and—totally unexpectedly—she found herself becoming a serious Christian. It happens. Her book *Traveling Mercies* chronicles her conversion.[1] A couple of years ago, Lamott published a book about prayer with the wonderful title, *Help. Thanks. Wow.*[2] According to Lamott, those are the three basic types of prayer. You're in trouble, and you're desperately looking for a way out—*help.* You are surrounded by gifts beyond measure, food and shelter, family and friends, the miracle that is each breath—*thanks.* And then there come those moments when you stand face to face with God himself, the Creator of the universe, the Mystery at the heart of all things, bathed in the light of eternal glory, and all you can say is—*wow.*

Now, I'm not sure that *all* prayers can be slotted into those three boxes. I suspect Lamott herself would admit as much. But it's not a bad place to start. So is our psalm for this morning, Psalm 10, a *help*, a *thanks*, or a *wow?*

Before answering this question, let's go back a psalm, to Psalm 9. Actually, scholars tell us that Psalms 9 and 10 are two halves of a single work. They're split up in our English Bibles, reflecting the Hebrew version, but in the Greek and Latin translations of the Old Testament, they are printed continuously. A quick skimming of Psalm 9 shows that it oscillates between *thanks* and *help.* This is one of the many psalms—actually, almost half of them—that bear the title "a Psalm of David." In it, King David gives thanks to God for delivering him and the people Israel from their enemies. He

1. Anne Lamott, *Traveling Mercies: Some Thoughts on Faith* (New York: Anchor, 2000).

2. Anne Lamott, *Help, Thanks, Wow: The Three Essential Prayers* (New York: Riverhead, 2012).

also praises God for being the protector of the poor and helpless. Defending the poor was one of the chief jobs of Israel's king, but even more so of *God* as the king. Near the end of Psalm 9, we read: "For the needy shall not always be forgotten, nor the hope of the poor perish forever." The rich and powerful don't care a fig about the poor, but God cares for them. Psalm 9 ends with an impassioned plea for God to not stop doing this—to rise up, and judge the nations of the earth, and keep on protecting the poor.

So Psalm 9 is mostly *thanks*, with just a hint of *help*. It looks back with gratitude, and looks forward with confidence. But what about its second half, Psalm 10?

Well, there's certainly no *wow* in it. That's something these two psalms have in common. But unlike Psalm 9, Psalm 10 has nothing to say about *thanks*. It's almost as if David's mention of the poor sets off a whole new train of thought. It dawns on him that while God may be the protector of the poor and helpless, the world doesn't *look* that way. In the world as we know it, God too often seems to be asleep on the job. And so David writes:

> [1] Why, O LORD, do you stand far off?
> Why do you hide yourself in times of trouble?
> [2] In arrogance the wicked persecute the poor—
> let them be caught in the schemes they have devised.

And so we can add another prayer to Lamott's list. Not just *help, thanks,* and *wow*, but *why. Why*, O LORD, are you so far away? Why do you hide yourself? It can't be that God doesn't care. Read the Psalms, read the whole Bible, and you will see that God is the special friend of the poor and the afflicted, the widow and the orphan, and in general of people who have no one who can advocate for them. Biblically speaking, that seems to be who God *is*. But then why, why, why does God allow the wicked to trample on the helpless and get away with it, time after time? Why doesn't God stand up and *do* something? And so we find ourselves face to face with the problem of evil. Wrestling with evil isn't just limited to the book of Job, with its profound meditation on the reality of suffering, or Ecclesiastes, which is sort of Stoic and philosophical about it. It's all over the Bible. There's hardly a page of Scripture that isn't haunted at some level by the question "why."

And David doesn't just ask why, but starts to wonder out loud about *they*—"they," of course, being the wicked. The first eleven verses of this psalm offer a penetrating analysis of how the mind of the wicked works. Maybe you have heard the slogan "the heart wants what it wants." If you're my generation, you may recall that Woody Allen said that to justify his own horrible behavior toward his wife, Mia Farrow. If you're younger, you may know it as a lyric sung by Selena Gomez. Actually, we can trace the words all the way back to a letter the poet Emily Dickinson wrote to a friend in 1862. The heart wants what it wants.

But before Allen, Gomez, and Dickinson there was King David, meditating on why bad people do bad things to vulnerable people. The reason is, they do it because they want to—their heart wants what it wants. Our psalmist doesn't use those words, exactly, but that's the basic idea. And because the heart wants what it wants, God be damned:

> 3 For the wicked boast of the desires of their heart;
> those greedy for gain curse and renounce the LORD.
> 4 In the pride of their countenance the wicked say,
> "God will not seek it out";
> all their thoughts are, "There is no God."

The words "There is no God" might suggest that the wicked are simply atheists, people who deny God's existence. But I don't think that's what the psalmist is getting at. It's not that God doesn't exist, but that God is absent, irrelevant, weak. Or maybe God just doesn't care. "There is no God" is the same as saying: "Okay, God, I'm going after my heart's desire—just try to stop me. I know you won't. I'm going to get away with it, because I am strong and you are impotent. Have your boring morality. I'm going out and have me some *fun*."

In the verses that follow, David looks on in horrified fascination as "they," the wicked, have their way with the innocent. It's as if he can't tear his eyes away. The wicked are utterly sure of themselves. They lie, they cheat, they steal, they curse God's name. They are like a beast of prey, a lion crouching at the door of its den and waiting to pounce. The prey of the wicked is not a gazelle or an antelope, however, but the poor. The ones the Bible says are God's special concern. But if God loves the poor so much, why doesn't God get up and *do* something?

Let's pause at this point and ask ourselves a rather dumb question. Who are the wicked? Who are these terrible people who mock God and trap the poor in their net and fulfill the evil desires of their evil hearts? Is wickedness always as obvious as the psalmist seems to think? How can we know who the wicked are?

Well, one thing we might do is ask the victims. The poor may not know everything about the people and systems that oppress them—it's very important that we not idealize the poor—but we can be pretty sure they will know *something*. It might even be that they will point the finger in our direction. One of the best modern commentators on the Psalms, the evangelical scholar John Goldingay, has said that Psalm 9–10 "speaks especially solemnly to powerful nations and especially encouragingly to weak ones. Most readers of this commentary therefore have to see themselves as the people who are being prayed against."[3] The same is likely true of the hearers and readers of this sermon. In the words of the famous comic strip *Pogo:* "We have met the enemy and he is us."

So maybe it would help us to be better readers of this psalm if, every time we see the words "the wicked," we instead read "the sinner." Because that's just what sin is—the denial of God, the mocking of God, the dismissing of God as irrelevant and out of touch. And because we Christians get to be sinners, we can know that we, too, have a hand in the evil that afflicts our world.

Wait—did I hear that right? Did he just say "we Christians get to be sinners?" What's that about? I thought sin was supposed to be bad? Well, of course sin is bad. But one of the great thing about being a Christian is that we have the privilege of *naming* our sin. Stanley Hauerwas has said that being a Christian is a matter of

3. John Goldingay, *Psalms, Volume 1: Psalms 1–41* (Grand Rapids: Baker, 2006), 184.

"learning to be a sinner."[4] By learning to name our evil actions as sin, we get sin out in the open, where it can be treated and healed. The tragedy of the people the psalmist calls "the wicked" is that by keeping God at arm's length, they are missing the opportunity for God to fix what ails them. God would deliver both the wicked and the poor, both the oppressor and the oppressed. But for that to happen, human beings have to stand still long enough to have *the truth* about them named. And the only one who can do that is the God who made and who loves us. This is why every decent Christian service of worship includes the confession of sin—and if I may boast just a little, we Anglicans have some pretty good ones.

I want you to notice how much our psalm is all about seeing and not-seeing. In the opening verse, the psalmist asks why God *hides* himself. In verse 8, the *eyes* of the wicked *watch* for the helpless. In verse 11, the wicked think in their heart, "God has forgotten; he has hidden his face; he will never *see* it." The sinner is sure she can get away with it, because God is far away up in heaven and doesn't *see.*

And that is why the turning point of our psalm occurs in verse 14, where the psalmist writes:

> But you do see! Indeed, you note trouble and grief,
> that you may take it into your hands;
> the helpless commit themselves to you;
> you have been the helper of the orphan.

But you do see! Can you hear the good news in that? God sees. God knows. God cares. These are convictions that run through the Bible from beginning to end. And I mean *literally* The End. In the book of Revelation, the Lamb, who is a symbol for Jesus, is said to have seven horns and seven eyes. The seven horns are a sign of his power, while the seven eyes symbolize "the seven spirits of God sent out into all the earth." Seven in the Bible is the number of completeness, the number of perfection. So to say that God has seven eyes or seven spirits means that God knows all things

4. Stanley Hauerwas, *The Peaceable Kingdom: A Primer in Christian Ethics* (South Bend, IN: Notre Dame University Press, 1991), 30–35.

perfectly. God is the ruler of history, and he is a wise and just ruler. God will see to it that the poor are vindicated and their persecutors judged for their evil deeds.

John the Revelator stands at the end of history, the psalmist stands in the middle. Yet he, too, shares John's fundamental trust that God will act to fulfill his promises. And so he writes:

> 17 O Lord, you will hear the desire of the meek;
> you will strengthen their heart; you will incline your ear
> 18 to do justice for the orphan and the oppressed,
> so that those from earth may strike terror no more.

These are the closing words of Psalm 10. They send us back to the beginning: "Why, O Lord, do you stand far off? Why do you hide yourself in times of trouble?"

When I was preparing this sermon, I did a very unscientific word search, to see how often the word "why" appears in the book of Psalms. I discovered that there are at least eleven other psalms where the psalmist challenges God head-on with the question "why?" Sometimes this happens more than once in a single psalm. And of course, it's not just the Psalms. That question runs like a red thread throughout the Bible. God's people cry out "why" to express their anger, or frustration, or bewilderment in the face of a God who seems to hide himself.

But at the heart of the psalmist's "why," the Bible's "why" is not anger or frustration, first of all, but love. It is because we Israel-people and church-people *love* God that his absence hurts so much. To be a Jew or a Christian is to love God, and to be pained at his absence. The Bible tells a love story—the church's life is a love story—and the question "why" is part of what it means to live that story. Of course, loving our neighbor is also a big part of that story, which is why, when we perceive injustice in our world, the rich and powerful exploiting the poor and helpless, we don't just pray, but *act*. I wish there were a better understanding in the church that praying and doing are not a zero-sum game. If we love God—and you wouldn't be here this morning if you didn't love him, or seek to love him—then we must love our neighbor also.

There is one who commanded us to love the Lord God with all our heart, mind, soul, and strength, and our neighbor as ourselves. It is his voice we hear in this psalm and in so many others—his voice that we hear resounding through all the length and breadth of Holy Scripture. But it's an ancient Christian tradition, going back at least to St. Augustine, that the Psalms speak with the voice of Jesus and of his body, the church.

Psalm 10 opens with the haunting question "why?"—"My God, why do you stand far off?" But Jesus was no stranger to "why." Hanging on the cross, he cried out "My God, my God, why have you forsaken me?" (that's from Psalm 22). But he is also the one who sees the plight of the poor and helpless. Was there ever anyone who saw, truly *saw*, his fellow human beings the way Jesus did? He saw the world as it truly was. He still sees it. He invites us to see the world through his eyes, without sentimentality or false hopes. It's a messed-up world in many ways, but also a world beloved by God.

Jesus sees. He sees *us*, and that's good news.

The psalmist cries out on behalf of the poor. Jesus is poor. So St. Paul writes to the church in Corinth that "you know the grace of our Lord Jesus Christ, that though he was rich, yet for your sake he became poor" (2 Cor 8:9). In one of his other letters, Paul even says that Christ emptied himself of his divine glory and honor, taking the form of a slave, and suffering a slave's death on the cross. Jesus' poverty is good news for us. It means we don't need to engage in the world's games of false status and power. We can be like Jesus—not necessarily literally poor (because, let's be honest, a lot of us are doing pretty well), but poor in terms of not accepting the world's hierarchy of values. He's rich. She's beautiful. They call the shots. The one who dies with the most marbles, wins . . . . Being a Christian means not playing the game by those rules. It means seeing other people not as means of advancement but as *human*—you'll notice I'm back to seeing things truthfully. I guess it must be pretty important.

Our psalmist is bothered by the success of the wicked, the ones who say in their heart "There is no God." Jesus knows there is a God. That sentence should win some kind of record for understatement. Jesus knows God? He is the eternal Son of the eternal Father. He knows God's justice, God's power, God's love from the inside. He knows that God *will* intervene on behalf of the oppressed. And so he taught his disciples to pray, saying, "Our Father, who art in heaven, hallowed be thy Name." He invites us to let his Father be our Father, and to cry out to God with him for the swift coming of God's kingdom on earth.

Let us pray. *Lord Jesus Christ, you do see. You see us in our weakness and terror. You see us in our secret sins. You see our need for God, and you bring us close to God. Help us to love God and one another. Give us the wisdom and patience to endure the things we cannot change, and the courage to change the things we can, trusting in you as our Lord and Savior. These things we pray in your holy name. Amen.*

CHAPTER XIII

Psalm 137

Happy dashers

Rev. Dr. Kate Sonderegger

Psalm 137

1 By the rivers of Babylon—
there we sat down, and there we wept
when we remembered Zion.
2 On the willows there
we hung up our harps.
3 For there our captors
asked us for songs,
and our tormentors asked for mirth, saying,
"Sing us one of the songs of Zion!"
4 How could we sing the LORD's song
in a foreign land?
5 If I forget you, O Jerusalem,
let my right hand wither!
6 Let my tongue cling to the roof of my mouth,
if I do not remember you,
if I do not set Jerusalem
above my highest joy.
7 Remember, O LORD, against the Edomites
the day of Jerusalem's fall,

how they said, "Tear it down! Tear it down!
Down to its foundations!"
8 O daughter Babylon, you devastator!
Happy shall they be who pay you back
what you have done to us!
9 Happy shall they be who take your little ones
and dash them against the rock!

Blessed are they who take your little ones and dashes them against the rocks.

I consider Psalm 137 the chief among the imprecatory psalms, the one most indigestible, and most shocking to our ears and to take on our lips. If we find a way to hear and to pray *this* verse, almost anything in Holy Writ will go down smoothly with us. I imagine that you have spent some time on this psalm, so I will hope to ring some changes on the themes you have already articulated.

Two words in the Hebrew text figure prominently in our exegesis: the Hebrew original for "blessed" or "happy" and the original for "dashes." Neither of these terms lessen our burden, but they do clarify some for us. One of the reasons this final verse from Psalm 137 unsettles and shocks us so, is that it begins, "Happy" or "Blessed" are they. This sounds like what exegetes call a makarism, that is, a blessing (from the Greek for blessedness).

That is what begins the Sermon on the Mount: Blessed are they that mourn. A makarism is a Divine passive: God is the agent who blesses, even if his Name is not pronounced. God blesses the poor, the persecuted, the grieving, the peacemakers. When our Lord speaks of these blessings in St. Matthew's Gospel, he intends for us to know that Almighty God blesses and keeps just those people, in just that way. It seems especially terrifying that God could bless those who crush children against the rocky ground, even the children of one's enemies. Happily, we can say that the Hebrew text does not turn this verse into a makarism: the Hebrew is not *baruch*, blessing by God, but rather *asher*—a very different term for readers of Holy Scripture! This kind of happiness is much closer to being led on a proper path, to find a straight route, to receive the happiness of a smooth road home. God does not give a blessing here; rather *the psalmist* does, and does so as a kind of victory lap. Now I don't think this makes our verse benign or palatable; far from it! But it does lessen the cord that constricts our heart when we think that God, the Just and Merciful, could countenance, could bless such terrible vengeance.

Now our second term, "dash," does not touch on such profound theological matters as does "blessed," but once again it clarifies just why this verse troubles us so, and should do so. *Naphats*—the Hebrew original—refers to an act of scattering, smashing to pieces, shattering the fragile into rubble. This is why we think in horror of a child's tender head being smashed, reduced to terrible shards, by the stones that inflict death upon them. This psalm has us recite the most devastating form of violence, brutality against the defenseless, the little one, the innocent.

Why should we recite such a verse? Why does it still stand in Scripture, in the Book we dare to call Holy?

I want to suggest to you a few reasons; but they are only a few, and they cannot fully satisfy. Perhaps nothing can do this. But they are reason before God, *coram Deo*, that I cling to when Holy Writ offends or terrifies or overwhelms me.

First, I have to consider how raw, how brutally raw and honest this verse truly is. The Psalter is unique in Holy Scripture as the Book not of God's words, but of *ours:* our prayers, our fears and longings, our thanksgiving and praise. And here the Psalter forces us to face honestly what we feel in our rage and shame and humiliation when we are taunted by those who flourish, whose ways are smooth and sleek, and who remain untouchable by their victims, the golden masters rolling by in their golden chariots. If you are like me, you have been raised and, we hope, formed by the Sermon on the Mount, and our Lord's teaching about the love of neighbor and especially the love of enemies. These are menacing words all on their own! But here they carry the odd effect of blinding us to our real and deep seated desire for revenge. Holy Scripture is ruthless in its realism and honesty. It will not let us hide from our deepest and most primal drives. Before our eyes it speaks the ominous truth—that our rage, too, our pain and jealousy and righteous anger, seeks expression in violence: Let the outrage be done to them that was done to me! We do not want to admit to ourselves that we desire just this kind of retribution; but Holy Scripture holds this mirror before us and demands we speak these terrible and unutterable words. The Holy God who looks on the heart sees these awful depths that we hid from ourselves. Scripture is the mirror in which we read our own truth. That's one response to Psalm 137.

The other is to consider the central place of wrestling, of striving, with Holy Scripture. I think we often consider the holiness of the Bible to be something like its pleasantness, its beauty and consoling moral depth, and do not often remember that holiness is not niceness. It is very far from it. Holiness has in the midst of its luminous glory a danger, an awe, a *tremendum*. To open the covers of the Bible is to uncover an explosive. The Word of God is not chained! There is nothing domesticated or predictable or soothing about this Book. That means, I think, that we are to *wrestle* with it. You remember that our ancestor Jacob was given the name Israel because he "strove with God" that night at the Jabbok (Gen 32:22–32). Verses of the kind we have been considering here tonight are the Night Season of Scripture. They are the dark places where we encounter the power of Holiness and we must strive with it till we wring from it a blessing. You remember that Jacob after his Night Season with Almighty God rose up lame. His socket was put out of joint by the blessing he demanded and was granted as dawn broke on that lonely morning. I think there is much good in every way in group Bible studies and in preaching to a full congregation; but in the end the Night verses must be encountered and wrestled to the ground by each one us, alone with our Holy God. Such a wrestling, as it did for Jacob, involves danger, and it involves repentance. Jacob properly feared meeting Esau, whom he wronged, and he, the wiley "man of many turns," finally came to see who he was in his brother's eyes—a small man, a broken one. But one who had seen the Face of God (Gen 33).

My own belief is that Psalm 137 should be read Christologically. This was certainly Augustine's deep conviction about the whole of the Psalter. Christ's voice speaks here, not only enunciating our own violent desires, but also offering himself as the Little One, the Innocent broken apart on the stony pavement, the rocky hill called "the Skull." We are indeed happy who know this Passion, this dreadful work of the Night, when the Sinless One became sin for us, hung until stone dead. It is terrible to think this and to read this verse in this way. But the death of our Lord is the great striving of all Scripture and of all history. And we the guilty, are the ones blessed by this crucified Child of God.

You will not read this verse as do I. But I commend it to you for your struggle, your deep encounter with vengeance, and with your striving for a blessing, this Night and in every Night Season that awaits you. May this Holy and Sacrificial God meet you there and bless you as dawn breaks!

CHAPTER XIV

Matthew 25:31–46

Why the end of time matters

Rev. Dr. Paul Scott Wilson

Matthew 25:31–46

31 When the Son of Man comes in his glory, and all the
angels with him, then he will sit on the throne of his
glory. 32 All the nations will be gathered before him, and
he will separate people one from another as a shepherd
separates the sheep from the goats, 33 and he will put the
sheep at his right hand and the goats at the left. 34 Then
the king will say to those at his right hand, "Come, you
that are blessed by my Father, inherit the kingdom prepared for you from the foundation of the world; 35 for I
was hungry and you gave me food, I was thirsty and you
gave me something to drink, I was a stranger and you
welcomed me, 36 I was naked and you gave me clothing,
I was sick and you took care of me, I was in prison and
you visited me." 37 Then the righteous will answer him,
"Lord, when was it that we saw you hungry and gave you
food, or thirsty and gave you something to drink? 38 And
when was it that we saw you a stranger and welcomed
you, or naked and gave you clothing? 39 And when was
it that we saw you sick or in prison and visited you?"

> [40] And the king will answer them, "Truly I tell you, just
> as you did it to one of the least of these who are members
> of my family, you did it to me." [41] Then he will say to
> those at his left hand, "You that are accursed, depart from
> me into the eternal fire prepared for the devil and his
> angels; [42] for I was hungry and you gave me no food, I
> was thirsty and you gave me nothing to drink, [43] I was
> a stranger and you did not welcome me, naked and you
> did not give me clothing, sick and in prison and you did
> not visit me." [44] Then they also will answer, "Lord, when
> was it that we saw you hungry or thirsty or a stranger or
> naked or sick or in prison, and did not take care of you?"
> [45] Then he will answer them, "Truly I tell you, just as you
> did not do it to one of the least of these, you did not do
> it to me." [46] And these will go away into eternal punish-
> ment, but the righteous into eternal life.

My invitation this morning was to be rude if I wished. I have never had that kind of invitation. It seemed too good to turn down. I checked the Oxford English Dictionary and the common meaning of "rude" is "uncivil, impolite, deliberately discourteous." But it has other meanings, two of which are of special relevance for us. Rude as a verb means to free someone of something, a variant spelling of the word rid. This is wonderfully true of the gospel, it frees us of something. And rude and its variant spelling, r-o-o-d, also means rod, crucifix, or cross. Our text today is very rude in all three senses—one of the rudest—and it's about what happens not at the end of summer but at the end of time.

At some point in the future, Jesus says, the Son of Man will gather all nations of the world before him, in all the colors of the rainbow. It will be like on the grade school playing field for sports, and everyone will be divided into two teams. The way Jesus tells it, this selection process promises to be no less painful than what the schoolyard was for some of us, when chosen last. The good team on the right will be called the sheep and the bad team on the left will be called the goats. The captain doing the choosing is Jesus Christ, who happens to be the captain of our souls. But Jesus chooses people not on the basis of their athletic ability, or their appearance, or their earthly success, or in this text—others are different—even on their doctrinal beliefs, but simply on their kindness.

Everyone wants to be on the sheep team because he says to them, "inherit the kingdom *prepared for you from the foundation* of the world; for I was hungry and you gave me food, I was thirsty and you gave me something to drink, I was a stranger and you welcomed me, I was naked and you gave me clothing, I was sick and you took care of me, I was in prison and you visited me." These acts presumably are not one-of-a-kind things or occasional events, for he chooses people on the basis of their habitual behavior, showing a disposition or attitude towards helping people. And Jesus rudely says to the unrighteous goats, "depart from me into *the eternal fire prepared for the devil and his angels*; for I was hungry and you gave me no food, I was thirsty and you gave me nothing to drink, I was a stranger and you did not welcome me, naked and you did not give me clothing, sick and in prison and you did not visit me." Both groups are amazed and respond in identical fashion, "Lord, when was it that we saw you *hungry or thirsty or a stranger or naked or sick or in prison, and did not take care of you*?" And to both he says, "Truly I tell you, just as you did [or did not] do it to one of the least of these, you did [or did not] not do it to me."

Most people, believers and non-believers, have at some time asked, "Will I be found good enough to enter heaven?" It is a fearsome question. Many of us guess we will not. We may say, "God can forgive others but not me, I cannot even forgive myself." At the last judgment there is no appeal because this is the court of appeal, the final court, the supreme court of God's justice. There are no degrees of guilt. Sheep right. Goats left. At least, that is how Jesus' words have been understood.

His words are such good news for so many people. Estimates hold that casualties in the Russian war in Ukraine may soon reach two million people. What good news is there for Ukraine if those responsible for this obscene horror were to escape punishment? But Jesus here promises that justice will come to them. Terrorists, rapists, murderers, racists, and pillagers of the earth around the globe and in our land, beware: Every life you damaged is precious in God's sight. We want justice to come and Jesus says that soon it is tally time, the accounts are due. Injustice and killing will not have the final say.

At the big checkout counter in the sky, every sin has a price. Every deed will be scanned. There will be a rude awakening for a lot of people. The guilty goats might hear these words, "You might have thought you could bank on your *good* deeds, but you won't have enough. Your fat wallet doesn't work here, and you won't have the currency to pay the price. You don't have enough bonus points on your charge cards, or enough rich relatives, or sufficient property to mortgage, or friends upstairs to help you out. You won't be to pay the price." It is gruff news for the goats—they cannot go home. Justice will be done. God will win. There will be a time when death and evildoers are no more. If we had an amen corner in church, the elders might be shouting, "That's right! Hallelujah! Amen!" And we might be joining them.

However, for most of us this good news is muted. There is a German word, *schadenfreude*, which means taking pleasure at the suffering of others. "The bad will get what is coming to them." But Jesus is not glad when people suffer, no matter how much they may deserve it. And God does not cause the suffering. Does God not weep when people choose the dead-end road instead of the path to life he sets before them? When they are given countless opportunities to say "YES, I choose you, Lord," they persist in saying "NO, no, no! to all truth, and goodness." We rejoice when those who do evil are stopped, but it does not change the continuing horror and suffering they leave behind and the sadness of their own wasted lives.

When we think of others getting their due, remember that we will all stand before God's judgment at that big checkout counter in the sky. There is only one lineup. There's no separate express lane for those with thirteen sins or less, no friendly cashiers who will ignore the odd sin here or there, no self-checkout lanes, and no special queue for terrorists, rapists, murderers, racists. We will all be in the same line. Who knows, we might all be looking around at each other's shopping baskets to see what is in there: "You said *that*?" "You did *that*?" When our own sins are scanned, truth be told, we will not be able to pay the price. We hope we have been good, but I know that I have willingly passed by some folks sitting on street corners with an inverted cap on the sidewalk who needed water, food, or shelter, and sometimes it did not even occur to me that it was Christ. I confess I haven't often gone out of my way to visit Christ behind bars. By the definition of our text, I am a goat. For various reasons, we are all goats.

Here is the problem: If every sin has a price, when the checkout register tallies what we owe, *none* of us will be able to go home to God. If all of the nations are divided into sheep and goats, the teams are not going to be even. There will be an endless multitude of goats on the goat side, folks who have done wrong, and the way I see it, over on the sheep side there will be one lone sheep. There will be only one who is innocent, and that is Jesus Christ, the one true sheep, the Lamb of God. One sheep and many goats.

I figure that Jesus already knew the composition of the teams when he told his parable. No sooner does he finish telling it, at the end of Matthew 25, than in the first two verses of chapter 26 he announces that the Son of Man will be crucified within the week. Why follow his parable with this announcement? In the parable he is the captain choosing the teams, and in the other, he prophesies his death next week. What is the connection? He is going to the cross to die. He is not just going to the cross to die, he is going to die *for the goats*. This is a rude surprise to many in his day, that the Messiah would die for his people. The idea is close to blasphemy. But Jesus came to save the sinners. Jesus says to the Pharisees in Matthew 9, "For I have come to call not the righteous but sinners." He includes them. He says, "Those who are well have no need of a physician, but those who are sick. Go and learn what this means, 'I desire mercy, not sacrifice'" (9:12–13).

To all who seek to follow him, Jesus freely grants acceptance. He gives a rude gift, rude in the sense of ridding us of something, in this case taking away our sin. He died for the goats. He became a goat for us—a scapegoat (Lev 16). He died for all the nations a rude death, a death on the rood or rod, a death on the cross. And on *Easter*—here is the amazing part—he rose again to sit at the right hand of God on behalf of the goats. He is God's judge. He is God's judgment. He is God's payment for our sins. He is the one who pays for us when we come up short at the checkout counter. He comes over to us who have done big bad or small bad, as we are vainly patting our pockets and purging our purses looking for the means to pay, and he says, "I see you are a goat. I am sorry. Goat, I love you. I love *you*. Let me pay for *you*. 'I desire mercy, not sacrifice.' Won't you let me offer you my cloak that you might share in my innocence and glory?" And for all of us who say "YES" to all that is truly good, he takes from our shoulders the goat's cloak of guilt, and trades it for his sheep's cloak. He drapes it over our shoulders that we might not only look like sheep but be counted as sheep by our God. If we bother to check the label, we will see that the cloak is 100 percent pure Lamb's wool.

If you want to take Jesus up on his offer, it is not too hard. Jane Glaves was from Brantford, Ontario. I use her story with permission. When she reached sixty-five, she went to Africa as a volunteer at an orphanage in Malawi where she tended to two-year-old twin boys who were badly malnourished. She got scabies from them, but she gave them health. When it came time for her to return to Canada and there was no one to care for them, she arranged with the help of many people, to bring them with her to Canada. So at sixty-six, she took on that responsibility. Her family thought she was crazy. Whatever she was, she was most certainly a sheep. We may not be able to go so far. All we need do is to offer bread and water, care and company. Be kind. Be kind. Be generous, not to become a sheep, for by God's grace you became that in your baptism, through faith. Rather, be kind because you love Jesus and you love doing God's will, and nothing about the future need cause you fear.

www.ingramcontent.com/pod-product-compliance
Lightning Source LLC
LaVergne TN
LVHW090526110826
845146LV00003B/997

* 9 7 9 8 3 8 5 2 6 0 2 4 9 *